PERFECT PARTIES

Now it's easy to make your next celebration an unforgettable success — just follow the simple plans in Perfect Parties! *This indispensable guide to creative entertaining has all the recipes and crafts you'll need for hosting get-togethers that truly have it all together. Whatever the occasion, you'll be ready with imaginative invitations, dazzling decorations, fabulous foods, and creative keepsakes. If wedding bells will soon be ringing, there's a tool-time shower for the groom and a lovely bridesmaids' luncheon strewn with fresh flowers. A little girl will feel like a princess at her dress-up birthday tea, and the birthday boy will have a roaring good time on a picnic expedition at the zoo! For your friends with football fever, there's a giant sandwich and lots of munchies for a great game-watching party. A little birdie helped us prepare the golfers' "par-tee" buffet featuring both "under par" (lower calorie) and "over par" (richer) choices. When the weather's nice, take the fun outside with a small garden supper, or invite the whole gang over for a cool pool party. As you turn the pages, you'll discover even more smashing ideas. Many parties have make-ahead recipes so you can spend more time with your guests, and each party offers a terrific opportunity for your creative talents to shine! With* Perfect Parties *to show you how, you'll enjoy the most rewarding part of entertaining — giving parties with your personal touch!*

Anne Childs

LEISURE ARTS, INC.
Little Rock, Arkansas

PERFECT PARTIES

EDITORIAL STAFF

Vice President and Editor-in-Chief: Anne Van Wagner Childs
Executive Director: Sandra Graham Case
Editorial Director: Susan Frantz Wiles
Publications Director: Carla Bentley
Creative Art Director: Gloria Bearden
Senior Graphics Art Director: Melinda Stout

DESIGN
Design Director: Patricia Wallenfang Sowers
Designers: Katherine Prince Horton, Sandra Spotts Ritchie, Linda Diehl Tiano, and Rebecca Sunwall Werle
Design Assistants: Sharon Heckel Gillam and Barbara Bryant Scott
Executive Assistant: Billie Steward

FOODS
Foods Editor: Celia Fahr Harkey, R.D.
Assistant Foods Editor: Jane Kenner Prather
Test Kitchen Home Economist: Rose Glass Klein
Test Kitchen Assistants: Nora Faye Spencer Clift and Leslie Belote Dunn
Contributing Foods Editor: Linda Adams

ART
Book/Magazine Graphics Art Director: Diane M. Hugo
Senior Graphics Illustrator: Michael A. Spigner
Photography Stylist: Karen Smart Hall

TECHNICAL
Managing Editor: Kathy Rose Bradley
Technical Editor: Leslie Schick Gorrell
Senior Technical Writer: Margaret F. Cox
Technical Associates: Briget Julia Laskowski, Kristine Anderson Mertes, Carol A. Reed, and Kimberly J. Smith

EDITORIAL
Managing Editor: Linda L. Trimble
Associate Editor: Tammi Williamson Bradley
Assistant Editors: Terri Leming Davidson Robyn Sheffield-Edwards, and Darla Burdette Kelsay
Copy Editor: Laura Lee Weland

PROMOTIONS
Managing Editors: Tena Kelley Vaughn and Marjorie Ann Lacy
Associate Editors: Steven M. Cooper, Marla Shivers, Dixie L. Morris, and Jennifer Leigh Ertl
Designer: Rhonda H. Hestir
Art Director: Linda Lovette Smart
Production Artist: Leslie Loring Krebs
Publishing Systems Administrator: Cindy Lumpkin
Publishing Systems Assistant: Susan Mary Gray

BUSINESS STAFF

Publisher: Bruce Akin
Vice President, Finance: Tom Siebenmorgen
Vice President, Retail Sales: Thomas L. Carlisle
Retail Sales Director: Richard Tignor
Vice President, Retail Marketing: Pam Stebbins
Retail Marketing Director: Margaret Sweetin

Retail Customer Services Manager: Carolyn Pruss
General Merchandise Manager: Russ Barnett
Distribution Director: Ed M. Strackbein
Vice President, Marketing: Guy A. Crossley
Marketing Manager: Byron L. Taylor
Print Production Manager: Laura Lockhart

Library of Congress Catalog Number 96-76037
International Standard Book Number 1-57486-008-9

Table of Contents

ANCHORS AWEIGH
POOL PARTY

Ahoy matey! You can make a big splash by hosting this cool pool party! Planned with a nautical theme and a menu of sumptuous appetizers, the good times begin with our hand-colored invitations, which feature nautical flags that signal "PARTY!" The buffet table, draped in red and white cabana stripes, is decorated with an assortment of "sea-sonal" accents, including shells, starfish, purchased lighthouses, and a signal flag party banner. For this carefree occasion, we chose lots of delicious foods that can be prepared ahead of time, like zesty Clam Cocktails and spicy Sailors' Snack Mix, and the fast-to-finish decorations take advantage of time-saving techniques. When the food's this good and the water's fine, all that's left is for your friends to dive in and have a wonderful time!

MENU

CLAM COCKTAILS

- 2 bottles (32 ounces each) vegetable juice cocktail
- 2 bottles (8 ounces each) clam juice
- 1/2 cup freshly squeezed lemon juice
- 1 tablespoon Worcestershire sauce
- 2 1/2 teaspoons celery salt
- 1 teaspoon hot pepper sauce
- 1 teaspoon grated onion
- 1/2 teaspoon ground black pepper
- 2 cups vodka

Celery ribs to garnish

Combine vegetable juice cocktail, clam juice, lemon juice, Worcestershire sauce, celery salt, pepper sauce, onion, and black pepper in a 1-gallon container. Stir in vodka. Cover and chill 4 hours. To serve, garnish with celery ribs.

Yield: about 13 cups clam cocktail

SAILORS' SNACK MIX

- 2 boxes (9 1/4 ounces each) pretzel mixture (containing large and small fish shapes)
- 1 box (10 ounces) sesame and cheese snack sticks
- 4 cups square wheat cereal
- 3/4 cup butter or margarine, melted
- 1/4 cup prepared mustard
- 2 tablespoons dried minced onion
- 2 tablespoons dry mustard
- 2 tablespoons Worcestershire sauce
- 1 teaspoon garlic powder
- 1/2 teaspoon ground red pepper

Preheat oven to 250 degrees. Combine pretzel mixture, cheese sticks, and cereal in a large roasting pan. In a small bowl, combine melted butter, prepared mustard, onion, dry mustard, Worcestershire sauce, garlic powder, and red pepper; whisk until well blended. Pour over pretzel mixture; toss until well coated. Bake 1 hour, stirring every 15 minutes. Spread on aluminum foil to cool. Store in an airtight container.

Yield: about 19 cups snack mix

SHRIMP COCKTAIL MOUSSE

- 2 envelopes unflavored gelatin
- 1/2 cup cold water
- 2 tablespoons freshly squeezed lemon juice
- 1 package (8 ounces) cream cheese, softened
- 1/2 cup mayonnaise
- 1/3 cup cocktail sauce
- 1 tablespoon grated onion
- 1 tablespoon prepared horseradish
- 1/2 teaspoon salt
- 2 cups (about 14 ounces) cooked, peeled, deveined, and chopped shrimp

Parsley and lemon slice to garnish
Crackers to serve

In a small saucepan, soften gelatin in water. Place gelatin mixture over low heat; stir until gelatin dissolves. Stir in lemon juice. Remove from heat. In a medium bowl, beat cream cheese until fluffy. Add mayonnaise, cocktail sauce, onion, horseradish, and salt; beat until blended. Fold in gelatin mixture and shrimp. Pour into a lightly oiled 4-cup mold. Cover and chill 2 hours or until firm.

To serve, dip mold into warm water about 10 seconds. Unmold onto a serving plate. Garnish with parsley and lemon slice. Serve with crackers.

Yield: about 4 cups shrimp mousse

DEVILED CRAB EGGS

1 dozen hard-cooked eggs, chilled
1 can (6 ounces) lump crabmeat,
    drained
1/2 cup mayonnaise
2 tablespoons finely minced sweet
    red pepper
1 1/2 tablespoons finely minced onion
2 teaspoons prepared mustard
1 1/2 teaspoons freshly squeezed
    lemon juice
1/2 teaspoon chopped fresh dill weed
1/4 teaspoon salt
1/4 teaspoon hot pepper sauce
1/8 teaspoon ground black pepper
    Fresh dill weed and chopped
      sweet red pepper to garnish

Cut eggs in half lengthwise. In a
medium bowl, mash egg yolks. Add
crabmeat, mayonnaise, red pepper, onion,
mustard, lemon juice, dill weed, salt,
pepper sauce, and black pepper to egg
yolks. Stir until crabmeat is broken into
small pieces and mixture is well blended.
Spoon yolk mixture into a pastry bag fitted
with a large star tip. Pipe yolk mixture into
egg white halves. Chill until ready to serve.
Garnish with dill weed and red pepper.

Yield: 24 deviled eggs

BLUE CHEESE AND PORT WINE SPREAD

1 package (3 ounces) cream cheese,
    softened
1/4 cup butter, softened
8 ounces soft, mild blue cheese, at
    room temperature
3 tablespoons tawny Port wine
1/4 teaspoon ground white pepper
3/4 cup finely chopped toasted walnuts
    Crackers and apple and pear slices
      to serve

Sweet, crisp apple and pear slices are the perfect complement to the piquant character of Blue Cheese and Port Wine Spread (clockwise from left). Prepared with crabmeat and sweet red pepper, Deviled Crab Eggs are delectable enticements. Shrimp Cocktail Mousse is a light, creamy version of a favorite seafood appetizer.

Process cream cheese and butter in a
food processor until blended. Add blue
cheese, wine, and white pepper; process
until well blended. Transfer to a small
bowl; stir in walnuts. Serve at room
temperature with crackers and apple and
pear slices.

Yield: about 2 1/4 cups spread

9

CHERRY TOMATOES WITH PESTO MAYONNAISE

1 cup mayonnaise
1 cup purchased pesto sauce
1 pint cherry tomatoes, halved

In a medium bowl, combine mayonnaise and pesto sauce; stir until well blended. Cover and chill. Serve with cherry tomato halves.

Yield: about 2 cups pesto mayonnaise

DOUBLE DILL DIP

1 cup coarsely chopped refrigerated kosher dill pickles
1 package (8 ounces) cream cheese, softened
1/4 cup sour cream
1 tablespoon fresh dill weed
1/8 teaspoon ground red pepper
  Fresh dill weed to garnish
  Corn chips to serve

Process pickles in a food processor until finely chopped. Add remaining ingredients and process until well blended. Cover and chill 2 hours. Garnish with dill weed. Serve with chips.

Yield: about 2 cups dip

HUSH PUPPY MUFFINS

1 cup yellow cornmeal
1/2 cup all-purpose flour
2 teaspoons baking powder
2 teaspoons sugar
1 teaspoon dried dill weed
1/2 teaspoon salt
1 container (8 ounces) sour cream
2 eggs
1/4 cup milk
1/4 cup vegetable oil
1/4 teaspoon hot pepper sauce
1/2 cup minced onion

You'll get hooked on these tasty surprises! Double Dill Dip (clockwise from top) blends refrigerated dill pickles and fresh dill weed in a cream cheese mixture. Shaped like little fish, Hush Puppy Muffins are corn bread treats flavored with dill weed, sour cream, onion, and a dash of hot sauce. Cherry Tomatoes with Pesto Mayonnaise are extra-easy appetizers!

Preheat oven to 425 degrees. Grease and preheat a 5-mold cast-iron fish-shaped muffin pan. In a large bowl, combine cornmeal, flour, baking powder, sugar, dill weed, and salt. In a small bowl, beat sour cream, eggs, milk, oil, and pepper sauce until well blended. Add to dry ingredients; stir just until blended. Stir in onion. Fill molds about 2/3 full. Bake 11 to 13 minutes or until edges are golden brown. Serve warm.

Yield: about 1 dozen muffins

ANTIPASTO PLATTER

Serve the following hors d'oeuvres with your favorite olives, cheese, and crackers.

PICKLED EGGPLANT

- 1 pound eggplant
- 1 tablespoon salt
- 1 cup water
- 1/2 cup white wine vinegar
- 2 teaspoons sugar
- 1/2 teaspoon black peppercorns
- 2 small cloves garlic
- 1 dried small chili pepper
- 1 sprig fresh oregano

Peel eggplant and cut into bite-size pieces. Place eggplant in a colander and sprinkle with salt. Allow to drain 30 minutes. Combine water, vinegar, sugar, and peppercorns in a Dutch oven over high heat; bring to a boil. Reduce heat to medium-low and add eggplant; simmer 8 minutes. Add garlic, chili pepper, and oregano to eggplant mixture; simmer 2 minutes. Remove from heat and cool. Cover and chill until ready to serve.

Yield: about 3 cups pickled eggplant

MARINATED VEGETABLES AND CHEESE

- 3 sweet red peppers
- 1 container (6 ounces) pearl onions, peeled
- 6 cloves garlic
- 1 pound Mozzarella cheese, cut in 1/2-inch cubes
- 8 ounces fresh mushrooms, cut in half
- 1 cup olive oil
- 1 tablespoon balsamic vinegar
- 3/4 teaspoon ground black pepper
- 1/2 teaspoon dried basil leaves
- 1/2 teaspoon salt

To roast red peppers, cut in half lengthwise; remove seeds and membranes. Place skin side up on an ungreased baking sheet; flatten with hand. Broil about

Add pizzazz to your party with a zesty Antipasto Platter! This appealing relish tray includes pickled eggplant, marinated vegetables and cheese, olives, and a cheese round.

3 inches from heat about 15 to 20 minutes or until peppers are blackened and charred. Immediately seal peppers in a plastic bag and allow to steam 10 to 15 minutes. Remove charred skin. Cut peppers into about 1/2 x 2-inch pieces. Set aside.

Place onions and garlic in a steamer basket over simmering water in a large saucepan. Cover and steam 10 minutes or just until onions and garlic are tender.

In an airtight container combine cheese, mushrooms, roasted peppers, onions, and garlic. In a small bowl, combine oil, vinegar, black pepper, basil, and salt; pour over vegetables and cheese. Cover and marinate overnight.

Yield: about 8 cups marinated vegetables and cheese

SPICY SAUSAGE ROLLS

Sausage rolls should be assembled and chilled the day before baking.

CRUST

  1 tablespoon sugar
  1 package dry yeast
  1/4 cup warm water
  7 tablespoons butter, softened
  2 eggs
  2 cups all-purpose flour, divided
  2 teaspoons dry mustard
  1 teaspoon dried minced onion
  1/2 teaspoon salt
     Vegetable cooking spray

FILLING

  1 pound Italian sausage
  1 green pepper, chopped
  1/2 cup chopped onion
  1 jar (2 ounces) whole stuffed green
        olives, drained, sliced, and
        divided
  1 cup (4 ounces) shredded
        Mozzarella cheese, divided
  1 egg yolk
  1 tablespoon whipping cream or milk

Baked in seasoned pastry, Spicy Sausage Rolls feature a meaty filling that includes Italian sausage, onion, green pepper, olives, and cheese.

For crust, dissolve sugar and yeast in warm water in a small bowl. In a large bowl, beat butter until fluffy. Add eggs, 1 cup flour, dry mustard, onion, salt, and yeast mixture; beat until well blended. Add remaining 1 cup flour; stir until a soft dough forms. Turn onto a lightly floured surface and knead 5 minutes or until dough becomes smooth and elastic. Place in a large bowl sprayed with cooking spray, turning once to coat top of dough. Cover and let rise in a warm place (80 to 85 degrees) 2 to 3 hours or until doubled in size.

Punch down dough in bowl and turn over. Cover and let rise in a warm place 1 1/2 to 2 hours.

Turn dough onto a very lightly floured surface and punch down. Shape dough into a ball and wrap in plastic wrap. Chill 1 hour.

For filling, cook sausage in a large skillet over medium-high heat until meat is browned; drain. Add pepper and onion; cook until vegetables are tender. Remove from heat; drain and set aside.

Divide dough in half. Roll out half of dough into a 10-inch square. Cut a 2-inch strip of dough from 1 side of square; reserve strip for decoration. Spread half of sausage mixture over dough to within 1 inch of edges. Sprinkle half of olives and half of cheese over sausage mixture. Beginning at 1 long edge, roll up jellyroll style; seal edge with water. Fold ends under and seal. Place sausage roll, seam side down, on a baking sheet. Roll reserved strip of dough into four 6-inch-long pencil-thin ropes. Cross 2 ropes over top of sausage roll near each end; seal with water. Repeat with remaining dough, sausage mixture, olives, and cheese. Cover and chill overnight.

Remove from refrigerator and allow rolls to stand at room temperature 1 hour. Preheat oven to 400 degrees. Beat egg yolk and whipping cream in a small bowl until well blended. Brush over dough. Bake 20 to 25 minutes or until crust is golden brown. If crust browns too quickly, cover with aluminum foil. Cool 10 minutes on pan. Cut into 1/2-inch slices. Serve warm.

Yield: 2 sausage rolls, about 14 servings each

OYSTERS BIENVILLE

1 cup half and half
2 egg yolks
¼ teaspoon salt
¼ teaspoon ground white pepper
⅛ teaspoon ground red pepper
¼ cup butter or margarine
¾ cup finely chopped fresh
    mushrooms
½ cup finely chopped green onions
    (about 6 onions)
3 tablespoons finely chopped fresh
    parsley
2 cloves garlic, minced
2 tablespoons all-purpose flour
⅔ cup white wine
½ cup shredded crabmeat or finely
    chopped shrimp
2 dozen fresh oysters on the half
    shell, drained
  Rock salt
¼ cup grated Parmesan cheese
¼ cup soft bread crumbs
¼ teaspoon paprika
  Lemon wedges to serve

In a small bowl, combine half and half,
egg yolks, salt, white pepper, and red
pepper; set aside. In a medium skillet,
melt butter over medium heat. Stir
mushrooms, onions, parsley, and garlic
into butter. Stirring constantly, cook just
until onions are tender. Sprinkle flour
over mushroom mixture. Stir constantly
until mixture is well blended; cook about
1 minute. Add wine; cook about 2 minutes
or until liquid is reduced by half and
mixture is creamy. Add half and half
mixture to sauce; stirring frequently, cook
5 to 10 minutes or until mixture thickens
and begins to bubble. Stir in crabmeat;
remove from heat and set aside.

Preheat oven to 375 degrees. Place
oysters on a layer of rock salt in a
10½ x 15½-inch jellyroll pan. Spoon
about 2 teaspoons crabmeat mixture over

Sailors and landlubbers alike will enjoy Spinach-Stuffed Seashells (left), oversize pasta shells baked with a cheesy spinach filling and topped with spaghetti sauce. Oysters Bienville are fresh oysters on the half shell topped with shredded crabmeat cooked in a rich wine sauce. The oysters are sprinkled with cheese and bread crumbs and baked on a bed of rock salt.

each oyster. In a small bowl, combine
cheese, bread crumbs, and paprika.
Sprinkle cheese mixture over crabmeat
mixture. Bake 20 to 22 minutes or until
tops are lightly browned. Serve
immediately with lemon wedges.

Yield: 2 dozen oysters

SPINACH-STUFFED SEASHELLS

3 tablespoons butter or margarine
¾ cup finely chopped onion
2 cloves garlic, minced
1¼ cups cottage cheese
⅔ cup grated Parmesan cheese
3 eggs
¾ cup seasoned bread crumbs
1 teaspoon salt
2 packages (10 ounces each) frozen
    chopped spinach, cooked and
    drained

1 package (12 ounces) jumbo pasta
    shells, cooked
1 jar (28 ounces) pasta primavara
    spaghetti sauce

Preheat oven to 350 degrees. Melt
butter in a small skillet over medium heat.
Add onion and garlic; sauté 5 minutes or
until tender. In a large bowl, combine
cottage cheese, Parmesan cheese, eggs,
bread crumbs, salt, spinach, and onion
mixture. Spoon spinach mixture into each
pasta shell. Place stuffed shells in 2 lightly
greased 9 x 13-inch baking dishes. Spoon
spaghetti sauce over shells. Cover and
bake 40 to 45 minutes or until shells are
heated through. Serve warm.

Yield: about 4 dozen shells

13

STRAWBERRIES AND CREAM

- 1 package (8 ounces) cream cheese, softened
- 1/2 cup sifted confectioners sugar
- 1 teaspoon almond extract
- 1 quart fresh whole strawberries, capped

In a medium bowl, beat cream cheese, confectioners sugar, and almond extract until smooth. Spoon cream cheese mixture into a pastry bag fitted with a medium star tip. Chill 1 hour.

Quarter strawberries from tip to stem end without cutting through stem end. Pipe cream cheese mixture into strawberries. Chill until ready to serve.

Yield: 1 quart stuffed strawberries

STARFISH COOKIES

COOKIES

- 3/4 cup butter or margarine, softened
- 1/2 cup firmly packed brown sugar
- 1/2 cup granulated sugar
- 1 egg
- 1 1/2 teaspoons vanilla extract
- 2 1/4 cups all-purpose flour
- 1/2 teaspoon baking soda
- 1/2 teaspoon cream of tartar

LIGHT TAN GLAZE

- 2 1/4 cups sifted confectioners sugar
- 3 tablespoons plus 2 teaspoons milk
  Brown and moss green paste food coloring

  Granulated light brown sugar and white non-pareils to decorate

WHITE DECORATING ICING

- 3 cups sifted confectioners sugar
- 1/4 cup vegetable shortening
- 1/4 cup butter or margarine, softened
- 1 1/2 to 2 tablespoons milk
- 1 1/2 teaspoons vanilla extract
- 1/8 teaspoon salt

  Granulated light brown sugar to decorate

These seaside surprises are sure to reel in compliments! Sweetened almond-flavored cream cheese is piped into succulent berries for our version of Strawberries and Cream (left), and granulated brown sugar makes a "sandy" decoration for buttery Starfish Cookies.

For our poolside decorations, we crisscrossed the table with colorful canvas to make quick-and-easy runners. A toy rowboat, a miniature gate, and other treasures from the sea are artfully arranged on a "beach" of granulated brown sugar. To make the maritime napkins, we simply hemmed squares of fabric, then placed them in canvas napkin rings that are embellished with figure-eight knots.

For cookies, trace starfish pattern, page 111, onto white paper; cut out. In a large bowl, cream butter and sugars until fluffy. Add egg and vanilla; beat until smooth. In a medium bowl, combine flour, baking soda, and cream of tartar. Add dry ingredients to creamed mixture; beat until a soft dough forms. Divide dough in half. Wrap in plastic wrap and chill 2 hours.

Preheat oven to 350 degrees. On a lightly floured surface, use a floured rolling pin to roll out half of dough to 1/4-inch thickness. Use starfish pattern to cut out cookies. Place 2 inches apart on a lightly greased baking sheet. Bake 7 to 9 minutes or until bottoms are lightly browned. Transfer cookies to a wire rack to cool. Repeat with remaining dough. Ice cookies with light tan glaze or white decorating icing.

For light tan glaze, combine confectioners sugar and milk in a small bowl; stir until smooth. Use a small amount of brown and green paste food coloring to tint glaze light tan. Ice tops of cookies and sprinkle with brown sugar or non-pareils.

For white decorating icing, combine confectioners sugar, shortening, butter, milk, vanilla, and salt in a small bowl; beat until smooth. Spoon icing into a pastry bag fitted with a medium star tip. Pipe icing onto tops of cookies and sprinkle with brown sugar. Store in a single layer in an airtight container.

Yield: about 1½ dozen cookies

15

ANCHORS AWEIGH INVITATIONS

For each invitation (page 6), you will need a 6³/₄" x 7" piece of white and a 3¹/₂" x 6³/₄" piece of red card stock paper; yellow, red, blue, and black permanent felt-tip markers with fine points; tracing paper; graphite transfer paper; stick glue; and a 5¹/₄" x 7¹/₄" envelope to coordinate with card stock papers.

1. For card, fold 1 short edge of white paper piece 2" to 1 side (front). Place 1 long edge of red paper piece into fold of white paper piece. Glue folded part of white paper piece to red paper piece.
2. Trace invitation pattern, page 110, onto tracing paper. Use transfer paper to transfer design to card.
3. Referring to pattern, use yellow, red, and blue markers to color design. Use black marker to outline flags, ropes, and letters.

SAILORS' GLASSES

For each glass (page 17), you will need a glass with straight sides (we used clear 13-ounce glasses); blue polyester canvas; ⁵/₁₆" dia. twisted cotton cord; craft glue; rotary cutter, cutting mat, and ruler (optional); and a hot glue gun and glue sticks.

Note: Remove canvas band from glass before washing.

1. (*Note:* We recommend using a rotary cutter to cut canvas.) Measure around glass; add 1". Cut a 2"w strip of canvas the determined measurement.
2. Overlapping ends, wrap canvas strip around glass; hot glue to secure.
3. (*Note:* To prevent ends of cord from fraying after cutting, apply craft glue to ¹/₂" of cord around area to be cut, allow to dry, and then cut cord.) For cord

decoration, measure around glass; add 6". Cut a length of cord the determined measurement.
4. Refer to Fig. 1 to tie a figure-eight knot at center of cord length.

Fig. 1

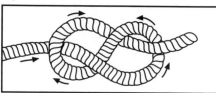

5. Wrap cord around center of canvas band and trim to fit so ends meet at overlap of canvas. Hot glue cord to canvas.
6. Cut a 1" x 2¹/₂" strip of canvas. Matching ends of strip to top and bottom of canvas band, hot glue strip to band, covering cord ends.

SIGNAL FLAG "PARTY" BANNER

For flag banner (pages 6 and 7), you will need ¹/₄ yd each of white, yellow, red, and blue 32"w polyester canvas for flags and appliqués; heavy-duty paper-backed fusible web; 2¹/₃ yds of ⁵/₁₆" dia. twisted cotton cord; white thread; rotary cutter, cutting mat, and ruler (optional); and craft glue.

1. (*Note:* Use a pressing cloth for pressing and fusing steps.) Press canvas on steam/cotton setting to pre-shrink.
2. (*Note:* We recommend using a rotary cutter to cut canvas.) For flags, cut the following 6" x 9" rectangles from canvas: 1 white, 2 yellow, 1 red, and 1 blue. For flag casings, press 1 short edge of each rectangle 1" to wrong side.
3. Follow manufacturer's instructions to fuse web to wrong sides of remaining white, red, and blue canvas.
4. For appliqués, cut the following pieces from canvas: one 3¹/₄" x 5" and one 2⁵/₈" x 6" from white; one 2⁵/₈" x 6" and

one 5¹/₂" x 6" from blue; and four 2¹/₈" x 3¹/₄", two 1" x 9", and two 1" x 4¹/₂" from red.
5. (*Note:* When assembling flags, refer to flags on invitation pattern, page 110, and fuse appliqués to right sides of flags.) Remove paper backing from appliqués. For "P" flag, fuse 3¹/₄" x 5" white piece to center of blue flag. For "A" flag, fuse 5¹/₂" x 6" blue piece to end of white flag opposite casing; cut an approx. 2¹/₂"-deep notch in blue end of flag. For "R" flag, fuse one 2¹/₈" x 3¹/₄" red piece to each corner of 1 yellow flag. For "T" flag, fuse 2⁵/₈" x 6" blue piece to end of red flag opposite casing; fuse 2⁵/₈" x 6" white piece to flag next to blue piece. For "Y" flag, evenly space 1" x 9" and 1" x 4¹/₂" red pieces diagonally on remaining yellow flag and fuse in place; trim edges of red pieces even with edges of flag.
6. For casings on flags, use white thread and a long stitch length and machine stitch ³/₄" from pressed edges of flags.
7. Thread flags onto cord. Knot and fray cord ends.

MARITIME NAPKINS AND NAPKIN RINGS

For each 19" square napkin and napkin ring (page 15), you will need a 20" square of fabric; thread to match fabric; polyester canvas to coordinate with fabric; heavy-duty paper-backed fusible web; ⁷/₈ yd of ⁵/₁₆" dia. twisted cotton cord; rotary cutter, cutting mat, and ruler (optional); and a hot glue gun and glue sticks.

1. For napkin, press edges of fabric square ¹/₄" to wrong side; press ¹/₄" to wrong side again and stitch in place.
2. Use a pressing cloth and iron on steam/cotton setting to pre-shrink canvas. Follow manufacturer's instructions to fuse web to wrong side of canvas.

3. (*Note:* We recommend using a rotary cutter to cut canvas.) For napkin ring, cut a 1³/₄" x 15" strip of canvas. Remove paper backing. Matching short edges, fold canvas strip in half and fuse together, using pressing cloth.

4. With folded end on top, overlap ends of canvas about 1" to form a ring; glue to secure.

5. Knot cord length about 2" from each end; fray ends.

6. Refer to Fig. 1 of Sailors' Glasses instructions, page 16, to tie a figure-eight knot at center of cord.

7. Centering figure-eight knot on canvas ring, glue cord to ring. Knot ends of cord together at back of ring.

8. Fold napkin as desired and insert into napkin ring.

SEASIDE SERVING BASKETS

For each basket, you will need ⁵/₁₆" dia. twisted cotton cord and a hot glue gun and glue sticks.

For lined basket (this page), you will *also* need a wooden basket with handle (our basket measures 9" dia. x 5"h) and 1 Maritime Napkin (page 16) to line basket.

For knot-trimmed basket (page 9), you will *also* need a shallow woven basket (our basket measures 16¹/₂" dia.), transparent tape, and craft glue.

LINED BASKET

1. For handle trim, measure length of handle; add 15". Cut a length of cord the determined measurement.

2. Refer to Fig. 1 of Sailors' Glasses instructions, page 16, to tie a figure-eight knot at center of cord.

3. Centering figure-eight knot at top of basket handle, glue knot to handle. Knot ends of cord at ends of basket handle; glue knots to handle. Trim and fray ends of cord.

4. Line basket with napkin.

Fashioned from twisted cotton cord, quick-and-easy figure-eight knots add nautical flair to our sailors' glasses and lined serving basket.

KNOT-TRIMMED BASKET

1. Using a small piece of tape on edge of basket to mark each section, divide basket rim into equal sections (we used the scalloped edge on our basket as a guide for marking 8 sections).

2. (*Note:* To prevent ends of cord from fraying after cutting, apply craft glue to ¹/₂" of cord around area to be cut, allow to dry, and then cut cord.) Measure length of basket rim between 2 pieces of tape; add 6". Cut 1 cord length the determined measurement for each section of basket rim.

3. For each cord length, refer to Fig. 1 of Sailors' Glasses instructions, page 16, to tie a figure-eight knot close to 1 end. Trim short end of cord close to knot (Fig. 1). Apply hot glue to back of knot to secure.

Fig. 1

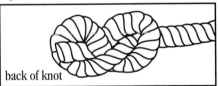

back of knot

4. Positioning knot of 1 cord length at each tape mark on basket rim, hot glue cord lengths to basket; do not glue knots to basket. Remove tape from basket.

5. Hot glue knot of each cord length over end of next cord length (Fig. 2).

Fig. 2

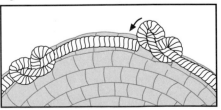

SUMMERTIME SUPPER

When the days grow longer and the warm nights are filled
with gentle breezes, it's the ideal time for an outdoor dinner
party for couples. Hand-delivered invitations, embellished
with pretty blossoms, set the stage for this informal social.
Inspired by Mother Nature, our table dressings include
fresh ivy, birdhouses, and bird nests. An antique bird cage
is filled with flowers and topped with a cascade of wired
organdy ribbons for an enchanting centerpiece. As guests
arrive, start the evening with citrusy Sangria Spritzers.
Our light summertime supper, which includes colorful
vegetable appetizers, a chilled soup, and a delectable steak
sandwich, will encourage easy, relaxed conversation.

MENU

For charming favors, place cards are set in handcrafted nests filled with foil-wrapped candy eggs. The whimsical napkin rings are made by attaching purchased miniature birdhouses to rings of ivy.

SANGRIA SPRITZER

- 2 liters red wine
- 1 can (6 ounces) frozen lemonade concentrate
- 1/3 cup orange-flavored liqueur
- 5 cups lemon-lime soft drink, chilled

Lemon and orange slices to serve

Combine wine, lemonade concentrate, and liqueur in a large container. Cover and chill until ready to serve.

To serve, combine wine mixture and soft drink. Serve with fruit slices.

Yield: about 15 cups spritzer

SALMON-STUFFED PEA PODS

- 1 package (8 ounces) cream cheese, softened
- 1 tablespoon finely chopped fresh parsley
- 2 teaspoons prepared horseradish
- 1 teaspoon freshly squeezed lemon juice
- 1 teaspoon Worcestershire sauce
- 2 cloves garlic, minced
- 1 package (3 ounces) smoked salmon
- 1/3 pound fresh snow pea pods (about 40 pea pods)

Process cream cheese, parsley, horseradish, lemon juice, Worcestershire sauce, and garlic in a food processor until well blended and smooth. Break salmon into small pieces; stir into cheese mixture. Remove strings from pea pods and slice 1 side open. Spoon filling into a pastry bag fitted with a large open star tip. Pipe filling into pea pods.

Yield: about 3 dozen pea pods

STUFFED BABY BEETS

- 2 jars (16 ounces each) small whole pickled beets, drained
- 1 package (3 ounces) cream cheese, softened
- 2 tablespoons minced sweet pickle
- 1 tablespoon minced onion
- 1 teaspoon freshly squeezed lemon juice
- 1/8 teaspoon salt
- 2 hard-cooked eggs, finely chopped

    Fresh dill weed to garnish

Scoop out a small portion of each beet with a melon baller; set beets aside. In a small bowl, beat cream cheese until fluffy. Stir in pickle, onion, lemon juice, and salt. Stir in eggs. Spoon mixture into a pastry bag fitted with a large open star tip. Pipe filling into beets. Garnish with dill weed.

Yield: about 32 beets

CHEESY CARROT BITES

- 2/3 cup shredded carrots (about 2 small carrots)
- 1 package (8 ounces) cream cheese, softened
- 1 cup (4 ounces) shredded Cheddar cheese
- 2 tablespoons chopped onion
- 1 tablespoon chopped celery
- 1 tablespoon Worcestershire sauce
- 1/2 teaspoon paprika
- 1/8 teaspoon ground red pepper
    Crackers
    Fresh dill weed sprigs

These pretty party pleasers are savory and delicious! Cheesy Carrot Bites blend shredded carrots with Cheddar and cream cheeses. Filled with a tasty cream cheese mixture, Stuffed Baby Beets are simply delightful! Salmon-Stuffed Pea Pods are flavored with garlic and parsley.

Process carrots, cream cheese, Cheddar cheese, onion, celery, Worcestershire sauce, paprika, and red pepper in a food processor until well blended. Spoon mixture into a pastry bag fitted with a large round tip.

To serve, pipe mixture onto crackers to resemble carrots. Place dill weed in large end of each piped "carrot."

Yield: about 4 dozen appetizers

CHILLED AVOCADO SOUP

- 1 medium cucumber, peeled
- 4 ripe avocados
- 3 tablespoons freshly squeezed lemon juice
- 2 medium green onions, finely chopped
- 2 tablespoons coarsely chopped fresh parsley
- 2 tablespoons salsa
- 1 to 2 cloves garlic, minced
- 1 teaspoon salt
- 1/4 teaspoon ground white pepper
- 3 1/2 cups chicken broth
- 1/2 cup plain yogurt
    Fresh parsley to garnish

Cut cucumber in half lengthwise and remove seeds. Slice half of cucumber and reserve for garnish; coarsely chop remaining half. Cut avocados into pieces and place in a food processor. Sprinkle lemon juice over avocados. Add chopped cucumber, onions, chopped parsley, salsa, garlic, salt, and white pepper; process about 30 seconds or until well blended. Add chicken broth and yogurt; process just until smooth. Place soup in a nonmetal container; cover and chill overnight.

To serve, garnish soup with reserved cucumber slices and parsley.

Yield: about 7 cups soup

FESTIVE CORN SALAD

DRESSING

    1 cup vegetable oil
   1/3 cup white vinegar
   1/4 cup finely chopped fresh cilantro
    2 tablespoons finely minced red
       onion
    1 teaspoon salt
   3/4 teaspoon ground black pepper

SALAD

    2 packages (16 ounces each)
       frozen whole kernel yellow corn
   1/4 cup water
   3/4 cup shredded carrots
       (about 3 small carrots)
   1/2 cup chopped red onion
   1/4 cup coarsely chopped fresh
       cilantro
    1 to 2 red jalapeño peppers,
       seeded and finely chopped

     Lettuce leaves to serve
     Avocado slices and fresh cilantro
       to garnish

Tied with gingham ribbon, little terra-cotta flowerpots are charming holders for bowls of Chilled Avocado Soup. A smooth, rich indulgence, the soup is prepared with ripe avocados and fresh cucumber. Bacon-Cheese Toasts are perfect soup-mates or appetizers.

BACON-CHEESE TOASTS

Spread may be made ahead of time and chilled.

    1 package (16 ounces) bacon,
       cooked and finely chopped
    3 cups (12 ounces) shredded
       provolone cheese
   1/2 cup mayonnaise
 2 1/2 tablespoons finely minced onion
    1 loaf (8 ounces) sliced white
       cocktail bread
    1 loaf (8 ounces) sliced wheat
       cocktail bread

Preheat oven to 325 degrees. In a medium bowl, combine bacon, cheese, mayonnaise, and onion. Spread about 2 teaspoons mixture on each slice of bread; place on an ungreased baking sheet. Bake 13 to 15 minutes or until cheese mixture is melted and edges of bread are lightly browned.

Yield: about 3 dozen toasts

Fresh cilantro adds distinctive flavor to Festive Corn Salad, a colorful vegetable medley.

Cumin, garlic, and jalapeño pepper spice up an oil-and-vinegar marinade for Southwestern Steak. The grilled meat is chilled and served on crusty Three-Cheese Sandwich Rolls with lightly sweet Creamy Mustard Sauce.

For dressing, whisk all ingredients in a small bowl until well blended; cover and set aside.

For salad, combine corn and water in a medium microwave-safe container. Cover and microwave on high power (100%) 10 to 12 minutes or until corn is tender, stirring every 3 minutes. Rinse with cool water and drain. Stir in carrots, onion, chopped cilantro, and jalapeño pepper. Pour dressing over corn mixture; toss to coat. Spoon over lettuce on individual serving plates. Garnish with avocado slices and cilantro.

Yield: about 10 servings

SOUTHWESTERN STEAK

- 1 cup vegetable oil
- 3/4 cup white vinegar
- 3 tablespoons finely minced red onion
- 1 tablespoon ground cumin
- 1 1/2 teaspoons sugar
- 3 cloves garlic, minced
- 1 red jalapeño pepper, seeded and finely chopped
- 2 pounds 1 1/4-inch-thick boneless top sirloin steak

For marinade, combine all ingredients except steak in a small bowl. Whisk until well blended. Place steak in an airtight container; pour marinade over steak. Refrigerate 8 hours or overnight, turning occasionally.

To grill, remove steak from marinade; discard marinade. Grill over medium-hot coals 6 to 10 minutes on each side or to desired doneness. Allow meat to stand 10 minutes. Place in an airtight container and chill.

To serve, cut cold steak diagonally across the grain into thin slices. Serve on Three-Cheese Sandwich Rolls with Creamy Mustard Sauce.

Yield: about 10 servings

CREAMY MUSTARD SAUCE

- 4 egg yolks
- 1/3 cup Dijon-style mustard
- 1/3 cup dry white wine
- 1 clove garlic, minced
- 2 tablespoons butter
- 1/4 cup sour cream
- 1 tablespoon honey
- 1/2 teaspoon chopped fresh tarragon leaves
- Pinch of salt

Combine egg yolks, mustard, wine, and garlic in the top of a double boiler. Whisk mixture over simmering water about 5 minutes or until thickened. Whisk in butter. Transfer to a small bowl; cool. Cover and chill 2 hours.

Stir sour cream, honey, tarragon, and salt into mustard mixture until well blended. Serve chilled or at room temperature with Southwestern Steak.

Yield: about 1 1/3 cups sauce

THREE-CHEESE SANDWICH ROLLS

- 1 package dry yeast
- 1 tablespoon sugar
- 1/4 cup warm water
- 2 1/2 to 3 cups all-purpose flour, divided
- 1 teaspoon salt
- 3 tablespoons butter or margarine, melted
- 2 eggs
- 1 cup ricotta cheese
- 3/4 cup (6 ounces) shredded Cheddar cheese
- 3/4 cup (6 ounces) shredded Monterey Jack cheese with jalapeño peppers
- Vegetable cooking spray
- 1 egg yolk
- 1 teaspoon water

A sassy combination of tastes and textures, Sour Cream-Lemon Cups layer smooth, tangy pudding with buttery lemon cookie crumbs. To carry out the garden party theme, place the dessert glasses in little terra-cotta saucers.

In a small bowl, dissolve yeast and sugar in warm water. In a large bowl, combine 2 1/2 cups flour and salt. Add melted butter, eggs, cheeses, and yeast mixture to dry ingredients; stir until a soft dough forms. Turn onto a lightly floured surface. Knead 3 to 5 minutes or until dough becomes smooth and elastic, using additional flour as necessary. Place in a large bowl sprayed with cooking spray, turning once to coat top of dough. Cover and let rise in a warm place (80 to 85 degrees) 1 hour or until doubled in size.

Turn dough onto a lightly floured surface and punch down. Divide dough into 10 equal pieces; shape into 2 x 4-inch rolls. Place rolls 2 inches apart on a greased baking sheet. Spray tops of rolls with cooking spray, cover, and let rise in a warm place 1 hour or until doubled in size.

Preheat oven to 350 degrees. Beat egg yolk and water in a small bowl; brush over rolls. Bake 20 to 25 minutes or until golden brown. Serve warm or transfer to a wire rack to cool completely.

Yield: 10 rolls

SOUR CREAM-LEMON CUPS

CRUMB MIXTURE
```
3   cups crumbled lemon cookies
1/3 cup butter or margarine, melted
1/4 cup sugar
```

PUDDING
```
2   cups sugar
1/2 cup cornstarch
1   teaspoon salt
3   cups cold water
6   egg yolks, beaten
1/2 cup butter or margarine
1/2 cup freshly squeezed lemon juice
2   tablespoons grated lemon zest
1   container (16 ounces) sour
     cream
     Whipped cream to garnish
```

Preheat oven to 350 degrees. For crumb mixture, combine cookie crumbs, melted butter, and sugar in a small bowl. Spread on a jellyroll pan. Bake 8 to 10 minutes or until golden brown, stirring after 5 minutes. Place pan on a wire rack to cool.

For pudding, combine sugar, cornstarch, and salt in a heavy large saucepan. Gradually stir in water. Stirring constantly over medium heat, cook about 17 minutes or until mixture boils and thickens. Stirring constantly, add a small amount of hot mixture to egg yolks; stir egg mixture back into cornstarch mixture in saucepan and reduce heat to medium-low. Gently stirring mixture, cook 5 minutes. Remove mixture from heat and stir in butter, lemon juice, and lemon zest. Pour into a heat-resistant medium bowl and continue to stir mixture about 3 minutes to cool. Place plastic wrap directly on surface of pudding and chill 30 minutes.

Fold sour cream into pudding. Spoon 1/4 cup pudding into each 8-ounce glass. Sprinkle 2 tablespoonfuls crumb mixture over pudding. Spoon 1/2 cup pudding over crumbs. Sprinkle additional crumbs over pudding. Garnish with whipped cream.

Yield: about 8 servings

BLOOMING INVITATIONS

For each invitation (page 18), you will need a 5³/₄" x 8¹/₂" piece of cream-colored card stock paper; assorted small silk flowers and leaves with stems removed; 1/3 yd each of 3/4"w gingham ribbon and 1¹/₂"w organdy ribbon, felt-tip pen with medium point, and construction paper to coordinate with flowers; brown watercolor pencil (sold where art supplies are found); small round soft-bristle paintbrush; tracing paper; graphite transfer paper; spray adhesive; and a hot glue gun and glue sticks.

1. Trace flowerpot pattern, page 111, onto tracing paper. Use transfer paper to transfer design to center of card stock paper with bottom of flowerpot about 1" from 1 short edge (bottom).
2. (*Note:* Practice using watercolor pencil technique on scrap paper before coloring project.) Use watercolor pencil to draw over transferred lines and shade pot, beginning with dark shading at left side of pot and gradually fading to very light shading at right side of pot. For pot shadow, lightly shade paper below and to the left of pot. For watercolor effect, wet paintbrush with water, blot brush on a paper towel to remove excess water, and paint over colored area as desired; allow to dry.
3. Hot glue leaves and flowers to paper at top of flowerpot.
4. Tie ribbon lengths together into a bow; trim ends. Hot glue bow to top of flowerpot below flowers and leaves.
5. Use felt-tip pen to write party information along edges of paper.
6. Use spray adhesive to glue decorated paper to construction paper. Trim construction paper to about 1/4" from edges of decorated paper.

BIRD NEST PLACE CARDS

For each place card (page 20), you will need natural excelsior, sphagnum moss, foil-wrapped candy eggs, a 1¹/₄" x 2³/₄" piece of cream-colored card stock paper, construction paper, felt-tip pen, gold paint pen, small twig (we used grapevine), spray adhesive, and a hot glue gun and glue sticks.

1. For nest, form a handful of excelsior into a nest shape. Fill nest with moss; hot glue to secure. Place candy eggs in nest.
2. For place card, use felt-tip pen to write guest's name on card stock paper. Use gold paint pen to draw a border on paper about 1/8" from edges. Use spray adhesive to glue paper piece to construction paper. Trim construction paper to about 1/8" from edges of card stock paper.
3. Hot glue place card to twig. Insert twig into nest; hot glue to secure.

BIRDHOUSE NAPKIN RINGS

For each napkin ring (page 20), you will need a purchased 2"h birdhouse ornament, 14" of fresh or silk ivy vine, a small bunch of fresh or silk flowers (optional), 1/3 yd each of 3/4"w gingham ribbon and 1¹/₂"w organdy ribbon, floral wire, and wire cutters.

1. Wind ivy into an approx. 2" dia. ring; wire ends to secure.
2. Wire hanger of birdhouse to ivy ring.
3. Loosely knot ribbon lengths together around ivy ring; trim ends. If desired, tuck flower bunch under knot of ribbon.

FOOTBALL FEVER

*When football fever strikes and the big game is on TV,
it's the prime time to throw a game-watching party! The
sporty invitations for this large-scale buffet are crafted
from card stock and paper napkin football motifs. As guests
arrive, they'll cheer for your spirited table decorations,
which include an old football, a helmet, and an arrangement
of fresh flowers embellished with a handmade pennant
and a multi-loop bow. The table runner and coordinating
napkins, made from football-motif fabric, are sure to
draw colorful commentary. And the hearty menu includes
treats like buckets of crispy, crunchy Championship
Snack Mix that will have fans running back for more.
Whether guests are cheering for opposing teams or
everyone's rooting for the hometown favorite, one
thing's for sure — this party spells V-I-C-T-O-R-Y!*

MENU

CHAMPIONSHIP SNACK MIX

24 cups popped popcorn
2 packages (12.3 ounces each)
   bite-size crispy corn-rice cereal
2 cans (12 ounces each) mixed nuts
2 cups butter or margarine
2 cups firmly packed brown sugar
3/4 cup light corn syrup
2 teaspoons vanilla extract
1/2 teaspoon baking soda

Preheat oven to 275 degrees. Evenly divide popcorn, cereal, and nuts into 2 large roasting pans; set aside. In a large saucepan over medium heat, combine butter, brown sugar, and corn syrup. Stirring occasionally, bring mixture to a boil; boil 5 minutes. Remove from heat. Stir in vanilla and baking soda (mixture will foam). Pour syrup over cereal mixture, tossing to coat. Bake 1 hour, stirring every 15 minutes. Pour mixture onto ungreased aluminum foil to cool. Store in airtight containers.

Yield: about 46 cups snack mix

TOUCHDOWN CHEESECAKE SPREAD

2 packages (8 ounces each) cream
   cheese, softened
1 cup finely chopped celery
1 medium green pepper, finely
   chopped
1 small onion, finely chopped
3 hard-cooked eggs, chopped
2 tablespoons freshly squeezed
   lime juice
1 teaspoon salt
1 teaspoon Worcestershire sauce
1 teaspoon paprika
1/4 teaspoon hot pepper sauce
1 1/2 cups crushed cheese crackers
1 1/4 cups thick and chunky picante
   sauce
   Crackers to serve

In a large bowl, combine cream cheese, celery, green pepper, onion, eggs, lime juice, salt, Worcestershire sauce, paprika, and pepper sauce. Spread mixture into a lightly greased 9-inch springform pan. Cover and chill 24 hours to allow flavors to blend.

To serve, remove sides of pan. Sprinkle top with cracker pieces. Spoon picante sauce in center of cheesecake. Serve with crackers.

Yield: about 6 1/2 cups spread

KICKOFF KABOBS

Allow enough time for kabobs to marinate.

1 package (9 ounces) uncooked
   refrigerated cheese-filled
   tortellini
1 can (14 ounces) artichoke
   hearts, drained and quartered
1 can (6 ounces) pitted ripe olives,
   drained
1 package (3.5 ounces) pepperoni
   slices (about 1 1/2-inch
   diameter)
   6-inch-long wooden skewers
1 bottle (8 ounces) Italian salad
   dressing
8 ounces farmer cheese, cut into
   1/2-inch cubes
1 pint cherry tomatoes, halved

Prepare tortellini according to package directions; drain and cool. Place tortellini, artichoke hearts, olives, and pepperoni on skewers. Place skewers in a 9 x 13-inch baking dish; drizzle with salad dressing, turning skewers to coat. Cover and chill 8 hours, turning occasionally.

To serve, remove skewers from dressing; add cheese cubes and tomato halves.

Yield: about 4 1/2 dozen kabobs

Start pregame activities with these spicy nibbles! Touchdown Cheesecake Spread (top) *drafts green pepper, picante sauce, and hot pepper sauce for a taste that's sure to score! Our Kickoff Kabobs team tortellini, pepperoni, vegetables, and cheese. Party lights with miniature football covers make fun table accents.*

SIDELINE SLAW

1½ cups mayonnaise
⅔ cup sugar
¼ cup apple cider vinegar
1 tablespoon salt
1 tablespoon celery seed
1½ teaspoons dry mustard
1 teaspoon ground black pepper
1 small green cabbage, quartered and cored
¾ pound carrots (about 7 small carrots)
4 medium zucchini
4 green onions, sliced
1 green pepper, cut into 1-inch-long slivers

In a small bowl, combine mayonnaise, sugar, vinegar, salt, celery seed, dry mustard, and black pepper until well blended. Cover and chill until ready to use.

In a food processor fitted with a shredding disc, shred cabbage and carrots. Transfer to a very large bowl. Cut zucchini in half lengthwise and scrape out seeds; shred zucchini. Add zucchini, green onions, green pepper, and mayonnaise mixture to cabbage mixture; stir until well blended. Cover and chill until ready to serve.

Yield: about 8 cups slaw

BAKED BEAN BLITZ

6 slices bacon
1 cup chopped onions
2 cans (28 ounces each) baked beans
2 cans (15.3 ounces each) lima beans, drained
1 cup barbecue sauce
¾ cup firmly packed brown sugar
2 tablespoons prepared mustard
1 tablespoon Worcestershire sauce
¾ teaspoon salt

Continued on page 30

Preheat oven to 300 degrees. In a large skillet, cook bacon; reserve drippings in skillet. Crumble bacon and set aside. Cook onions in bacon drippings until tender. In a 9 x 13-inch baking dish, combine onions and drippings with beans, barbecue sauce, brown sugar, mustard, Worcestershire sauce, and salt. Stirring occasionally, bake about 2 hours. To serve, stir in bacon. Serve warm.

Yield: about 10 servings

FIELD GOAL POTATOES

  3 pounds unpeeled red potatoes, cut into chunks
  6 tablespoons vegetable oil
  2 packages (1¼ ounces each) cheese sauce mix
  1 can (4.5 ounces) chopped green chiles
  3 tablespoons dried minced onion
  1 tablespoon ground cumin
  1 tablespoon garlic powder
1½ teaspoons salt
  ¾ teaspoon dried cilantro

Preheat oven to 450 degrees. Place potatoes in a large bowl. In a small bowl, whisk oil and cheese sauce mix until well blended. Stir green chiles, onion, cumin, garlic powder, salt, and cilantro into cheese mixture. Pour mixture over potatoes, stirring until potatoes are well coated. Spread potato mixture in a single layer in a greased 10½ x 15½-inch jellyroll pan. Bake 35 to 45 minutes or until potatoes are tender and golden brown. Serve warm.

Yield: about 12 servings

Your guests will huddle around the buffet for a taste of these first-round side-dish picks! Field Goal Potatoes (clockwise from bottom) are cheesy chunks flavored with green chiles, cumin, and cilantro. Tangy Baked Bean Blitz will have them cheering for more, and zucchini adds extra points to Sideline Slaw. For all-star wide receivers, the snack trays are lined with artificial turf.

Our super Stadium Sandwich is large enough to satisfy the whole team! Piled high on a football-shaped roll, this hero makes a power play for taste with salami, ham, turkey, and a backfield of fresh, crispy veggies. Giant football confetti glued to skewers tackle the job of holding sandwich servings together.

STADIUM SANDWICH

Vegetable cooking spray
1 package (16 ounces) hot roll mix
1 cup hot water
1 egg
2 tablespoons butter or margarine, softened
1/2 cup purchased sandwich spread
6 lettuce leaves
1/2 cucumber, thinly sliced
1/2 green pepper, thinly sliced
1 red onion, sliced and separated into rings
5 ounces sliced American cheese
5 ounces sliced Swiss cheese
8 ounces sliced salami
8 ounces sliced ham
5 ounces sliced Colby cheese
8 ounces sliced turkey
1 tomato, thinly sliced
6-inch-long wooden skewers to serve

Spray a 12 x 7³/₄ x 3-inch-deep football-shaped cake pan with cooking spray. Prepare hot roll mix according to package directions using hot water, egg, and butter. After the 5-minute rest, press dough into prepared pan. Cover and let rise in a warm place (80 to 85 degrees) about 30 minutes or until doubled in size.

Preheat oven to 375 degrees. To keep bread flat, place a baking sheet on top of football pan; place a heavy ovenproof pan on baking sheet. Bake 20 minutes; remove baking sheet from football pan. Bake bread an additional 3 to 5 minutes or until lightly browned. Cool in pan on a wire rack 5 minutes. Remove bread from pan and cool completely on wire rack.

To serve, cut bread in half horizontally. Spread cut sides of bread with sandwich spread. Layer lettuce, cucumber, green pepper, onion, American cheese, Swiss cheese, salami, ham, Colby cheese, turkey, and tomato slices on bottom half of bread. Replace top of bread. Cut sandwich crosswise into 3-inch slices; cut each slice into about 2¹/₂-inch-long pieces and secure with skewers. Serve immediately.

Yield: about 10 servings

TIME-OUT MACADAMIA COOKIES

½ cup butter or margarine, softened
½ cup vegetable shortening
¾ cup firmly packed brown sugar
½ cup granulated sugar
1 egg
1½ teaspoons vanilla extract
2 cups all-purpose flour
1 teaspoon baking soda
½ teaspoon salt
1 package (6 ounces) white baking chocolate, cut into chunks
1 jar (7 ounces) macadamia nuts, coarsely chopped

Preheat oven to 350 degrees. In a large bowl, cream butter, shortening, and sugars until fluffy. Add egg and vanilla; beat until smooth. In a medium bowl, combine flour, baking soda, and salt. Add dry ingredients to creamed mixture; stir until a soft dough forms. Stir in white chocolate and macadamia nuts. Drop teaspoonfuls of dough 2 inches apart onto an ungreased baking sheet. Bake 8 to 10 minutes or until lightly browned. Transfer cookies to a wire rack to cool. Store in an airtight container.

Yield: about 4½ dozen cookies

QUARTERBACK SNEAK BROWNIES

1 package (18.25 ounces) German chocolate cake mix with pudding in the mix
⅔ cup butter or margarine, melted
⅔ cup evaporated milk, divided
½ cup pecans, chopped
1 package (14 ounces) caramels
1 package (6 ounces) semisweet chocolate chips

Champions of the "Dessert Bowl," Quarterback Sneak Brownies and Time-out Macadamia Cookies are record-breaking taste sensations. By drafting creamy caramels, chunky white chocolate, and buttery rich nuts, these chewy treats are crowd pleasers! A shoo-in for MVP (Most Valuable Party favors), our quick-snap coolers will defend against water rings and warm beverages.

Preheat oven to 350 degrees. In a medium bowl, combine cake mix, butter, ⅓ cup evaporated milk, and pecans. Spread half of mixture into a greased 9 x 13-inch baking pan; reserve remaining mixture. Bake 10 minutes or until slightly firm; set aside.

Microwave caramels and remaining ⅓ cup evaporated milk in a 2-quart microwave-safe dish on medium power (50%) 5 to 7 minutes or until caramels melt, stirring after 3 minutes. Sprinkle chocolate chips over cake; spread melted caramel mixture over chocolate chips. Break up reserved cake mix mixture and drop over top of cake; bake 20 to 24 minutes or until almost set. Cool brownies; cut into 2-inch squares. Store in an airtight container.

Yield: about 2 dozen brownies

KICKOFF INVITATIONS

For each invitation (page 26), you will need a 6¼" x 8⅝" piece of 1 color of card stock paper and a 4⅝" x 6¼" piece of a second color of card stock paper (we used green and yellow), paper napkin or fabric with football motif(s), black permanent felt-tip pen with fine point, spray adhesive, and an approx. 4¾" x 6½" envelope to coordinate with card stock paper.

1. For card, use spray adhesive to glue small paper piece to 1 end of large paper piece, matching edges.
2. Fold uncovered part of large paper piece to front over small paper piece.
3. Cut football motif(s) from napkin. Use spray adhesive to glue motif(s) to front of card.
4. Use black pen to write "FOOTBALL FEVER!!!" across exposed area of small paper piece.

CENTERPIECE PENNANT

For pennant (page 27), you will need one 5" x 9" piece each of 2 different colors of card stock paper (we used yellow and green), 18" of 5/16" dia. wooden dowel, black permanent felt-tip pen with fine point, tracing paper, graphite transfer paper, and a hot glue gun and glue sticks.

1. Trace pennant pattern, page 112, onto tracing paper; cut out pattern along outer lines.
2. Use pattern to cut 1 pennant shape from each color of card stock paper.
3. Use transfer paper to transfer "GO TEAM!" onto 1 pennant shape. Use black pen to color letters.
4. Extending point of remaining shape about ⅝" beyond point of first shape, use small dots of glue to glue remaining

pennant shape to back of first pennant shape.
5. Wrap and glue short edge of pennant around 1 end of dowel.
6. Insert pennant in a fall floral arrangement.

TOUCHDOWN TABLE GEAR

For table runner (pages 26 and 27), you will need football-motif fabric (we used NFL™ fabric by Fabric Traditions), thread to match fabric, ⅝"w grosgrain ribbon, and washable fabric glue.
For each 18" square napkin (page 27), you will need a 19" square of fabric to match table runner, thread to match fabric, and two ⅔ yd lengths of ⅛"w grosgrain ribbon and ⅔ yd of ⅝"w satin ribbon to coordinate with fabric.

TABLE RUNNER
1. Cut a piece of fabric ½" larger on all sides than desired finished size of runner (the fabric piece for our runner measured 17½" x 59").
2. Press long edges, then short edges of fabric piece ¼" to wrong side; press ¼" to wrong side again and stitch in place.
3. For trim, measure 1 long edge of runner. Cut 2 lengths of ribbon the determined measurement. Glue 1 ribbon length along each long edge on right side of runner. Repeat to glue ribbon lengths along short edges of runner.

NAPKIN
1. Press edges of fabric square ¼" to wrong side; press ¼" to wrong side again and stitch in place.
2. Fold napkin as desired. Tie ribbon lengths together into bow around napkin; trim ribbon ends.

"GO TEAM!" SNACK BUCKETS

For each bucket (page 27), you will need an approx. 6" dia. x 4½"h chipwood bucket with wire handle, either a 15" square of football-motif fabric (we used NFL™ fabric by Fabric Traditions) or a large napkin to line bucket, card stock paper to coordinate with fabric, black permanent felt-tip pen with fine point, transparent tape (if needed), and a hot glue gun and glue sticks.

1. Measure width of bucket rim. Measure around bucket rim; add 1". Cut a strip of paper the determined measurements, piecing with tape as necessary.
2. Use black pen to write "GO TEAM!" several times along paper strip.
3. Overlapping ends, glue strip around bucket rim.
4. Line bucket with fabric square.

FIRST DOWN SNACK TRAYS

Our sturdy snack trays (page 27) allow guests to move "down the field" with ease from the buffet to their game-watching seats. Each approx. 13" x 19" bamboo tray is lined with green artificial turf (available at hardware stores). Simply draw around bottom of tray on wrong side of turf and use utility scissors to cut out shape, trimming as necessary to fit in bottom of tray.

QUARTERBACK SNAP COOLERS

For each cooler (page 32), take apart a Crafter's Pride® Stitch-A-Cooler™ (available at craft stores) and set Vinyl Weave™ insert aside for another use. Cut a 4" x 10" piece from either a paper napkin or fabric with a football motif. Overlapping short edges, use craft glue to glue napkin piece around foam insulator from cooler. Reassemble cooler.

GOLFERS' "PAR-TEE"

A little birdie told us that a fun-filled party for golfers would be a great way to relax at the 19th hole! The hand-colored invitations announce that this is "A Par-Tee Just Fore Fun!" The menu for the buffet-style gathering features foods that everyone can enjoy, with a choice of "under par" (lower calorie) and "over par" (richer) offerings. Upon arrival, your fairway friends will applaud the pristine course tabletop, complete with plaid accents and a felt "green." Arrangements of potted grass and misplayed balls are reminders that golf can be a "rough" sport! To carry out the theme, place card flags are created using practice putting cups, and seat covers are cut from artificial turf and tied to chairs using lengths of plaid ribbon. To keep everyone in the swing of things, serve Tee-Time Apricot Sours and Onion Focaccia drizzled with Rosemary-Flavored Oil. While the gallery discusses handicaps, strokes, and the hazards of the game, encourage them to relax and have a good time — just "fore" the fun of it!

Our "Under Par" (lower calorie) selections are marked with flags for easy reference.

MENU

Tee-Time Apricot Sours

Onion Focaccia

Rosemary-Flavored Oil

Spinach and Kale Soup

Parmesan Croutons

Manicured Greens

Parmesan Vinaigrette

Creamy Garlic Dressing

Herbed Salmon

Lemon Pasta

Tomato and Basil Salsa

Mustard-Caper Cream Sauce

Poppy Seed Rosettes

Cracked Pepper Butter

Chocolate Meringue Sandtraps with Creamy Orange Filling

Golf Ball Truffles

TEE-TIME APRICOT SOURS

  4 cans (11.5 ounces each) apricot nectar
  2 cups water
  1 can (12 ounces) frozen lemonade concentrate, thawed
 1/4 cup grenadine syrup
    Lemon slices to serve

In a large container, combine apricot nectar, water, lemonade concentrate, and grenadine syrup. Cover and chill until ready to serve. To serve, add a lemon slice to each serving.

Yield: about 9 cups sours

OVER PAR VERSION: Add 1 1/2 cups apricot brandy and 1/2 cup amaretto to Tee-Time Apricot Sours to yield about 11 cups sours.

ONION FOCACCIA

Prepare onions while dough is rising.

  1 package dry yeast
  1 teaspoon sugar
 1 1/2 cups warm water
  4 teaspoons olive oil, divided
 3 1/2 to 4 cups all-purpose flour, divided
 1 1/2 teaspoons salt, divided
    Vegetable cooking spray
 1 1/2 pounds onions
  1 tablespoon finely chopped fresh rosemary leaves
 1/2 teaspoon ground black pepper
  1 package (7 ounces) feta cheese
    Rosemary-Flavored Oil to serve

In a small bowl, dissolve yeast and sugar in warm water. Stir in 3 teaspoons oil. In a large bowl, combine 3 cups flour and 1 teaspoon salt. Add yeast mixture to dry ingredients; stir until a soft dough forms. Turn onto a lightly floured surface.

Knead about 5 minutes or until dough becomes smooth and elastic, using additional flour as necessary. Place in a large bowl sprayed with cooking spray, turning once to coat top of dough. Cover and let rise in a warm place (80 to 85 degrees) 1 1/2 hours or until doubled in size.

Turn dough onto a lightly floured surface and punch down. Cover and allow dough to rest 10 minutes. Divide dough in half. Press each half into a 9-inch-diameter circle on a lightly greased baking sheet. Brush dough circles with remaining 1 teaspoon oil. Cover with plastic wrap and let rise in a warm place 30 minutes.

Preheat oven to 350 degrees. Cut each onion into 8 wedges. Place in a 9 x 13-inch baking pan sprayed with cooking spray. Lightly spray onions with cooking spray and sprinkle with rosemary, remaining 1/2 teaspoon salt, and pepper. Cover and bake 45 minutes. Uncover and bake 45 minutes to 1 hour or until onions are lightly browned.

Increase temperature to 425 degrees. Place baked onions on dough. Crumble cheese over onions. Bake 16 to 20 minutes or until crust is golden brown. Cut into 2-inch squares and serve warm with Rosemary-Flavored Oil.

Yield: 2 focaccia rounds, 16 to 18 pieces each

ROSEMARY-FLAVORED OIL

  1 cup olive oil
  1 teaspoon minced fresh rosemary leaves
  4 small fresh rosemary sprigs

Combine oil and minced rosemary in a glass container. Cover and allow to sit 8 hours. Strain and discard rosemary. Place rosemary sprigs in a decorative bottle. Pour flavored oil into bottle. Store in refrigerator up to 10 days. To serve, drizzle over Onion Foccacia.

Yield: 1 cup flavored oil

SPINACH AND KALE SOUP

1½ cups finely chopped onion
    (about 1 large onion)
  3 tablespoons vegetable oil
  2 cloves garlic, minced
  4 cans (14½ ounces each)
    chicken broth
  1 pound fresh spinach, washed,
    drained, stemmed, and chopped
  1 pound fresh kale, washed,
    drained, stemmed, and chopped
  2 medium potatoes, cubed
  2 medium carrots, thinly sliced
  1 tablespoon freshly squeezed
    lemon juice
 ¾ teaspoon salt
 ¼ teaspoon ground black pepper

In a stockpot, sauté onion in oil over medium heat until soft. Add garlic; sauté 2 to 3 minutes or until garlic and onion begin to brown. Stir in chicken broth. Increase heat to medium-high and add spinach, kale, potatoes, and carrots; cover and bring mixture to a boil. Reduce heat to medium-low; cook about 15 minutes or until vegetables are tender. Stir in lemon juice, salt, and pepper. Serve warm.

Yield: about 11½ cups soup

OVER PAR VERSION: Serve Spinach and Kale Soup with Parmesan Croutons and crumbled bacon.

Chicken broth brings out the savory goodness of Spinach and Kale Soup, which is prepared with fresh greens, carrots, and potatoes. For added flavor, serve the soup with Parmesan Croutons and crisp bacon.

PARMESAN CROUTONS

¼ cup freshly grated Parmesan cheese
 6 tablespoons olive oil
½ teaspoon garlic salt
¼ teaspoon ground white pepper
 4 cups of ¾-inch cubes day-old
   French bread

Place cheese in a large bowl. In a large skillet, heat oil, garlic salt, and white pepper over medium heat; stir until well blended. Stir in bread cubes. Stirring frequently, cook bread 12 to 15 minutes or until golden brown. Toss bread cubes in cheese until well coated. Cool to room temperature. Store in an airtight container. Serve with Spinach and Kale Soup.

Yield: about 3 cups croutons

CREAMY GARLIC DRESSING

2 cups mayonnaise
¹/₂ cup sour cream
¹/₄ cup freshly grated Parmesan cheese
4 to 5 cloves garlic, minced
1 tablespoon white wine vinegar
1 tablespoon freshly squeezed
    lemon juice
1 teaspoon Dijon-style mustard
¹/₂ teaspoon salt
¹/₄ teaspoon ground white pepper
¹/₃ cup half and half

In a medium bowl, whisk mayonnaise, sour cream, cheese, garlic, vinegar, lemon juice, mustard, salt, and white pepper until well blended. Whisk in half and half. Cover and chill 4 hours to allow flavors to blend. Serve with Manicured Greens.

Yield: about 3 cups dressing

HERBED SALMON

Vegetable cooking spray
2 pounds fresh salmon fillet, cut
    into eight 4-ounce servings
¹/₃ cup reduced-calorie mayonnaise
2 tablespoons minced onion
1 tablespoon finely chopped fresh
    parsley
2 teaspoons white wine
    Worcestershire sauce
¹/₂ teaspoon salt
¹/₄ teaspoon ground white pepper

Preheat oven to 425 degrees. Spray a 9 x 13-inch baking pan with cooking spray. Place salmon, skin side down, in prepared pan. In a small bowl, combine mayonnaise, onion, parsley, Worcestershire sauce, salt, and white pepper; stir until well blended. Spread about 1 tablespoon mixture over top of each salmon piece. Bake 12 to 15 minutes or until fish flakes easily. Serve warm.

Yield: 8 servings

Paired with Creamy Garlic Dressing (right) *or tangy Parmesan Vinaigrette, Manicured Greens is a luscious salad. The "hole-in-one" serving bowls are encircled with bands of plaid fabric and labeled with an "Over Par" or "Under Par" flag. Embellished with familiar golfing terms, the "pro tour" salad bowl stand is mounted on golf balls.*

MANICURED GREENS

10 to 12 cups torn assorted salad
    greens (we used escarole and
    red leaf and green leaf lettuce)
4 to 5 plum tomatoes, sliced
1 sweet red pepper, sliced into
    1-inch-long matchstick pieces
1 to 2 cucumbers, sliced
1 to 2 carrots, sliced
    Parmesan Vinaigrette or Creamy
    Garlic Dressing to serve

Toss salad greens, tomatoes, red pepper, cucumbers, and carrots in a large serving bowl. Serve with Parmesan Vinaigrette or Creamy Garlic Dressing.

Yield: 12 to 14 servings

PARMESAN VINAIGRETTE

¹/₂ cup red wine vinegar
6 tablespoons freshly grated
    Parmesan cheese
3 tablespoons balsamic vinegar
2 tablespoons Dijon-style mustard
2 cloves garlic, minced
³/₄ teaspoon salt
¹/₂ teaspoon ground black pepper

For vinaigrette, place all ingredients in a blender; cover and blend until smooth. Pour into a small bowl; cover and let stand at room temperature 4 hours to allow flavors to blend. Serve with Manicured Greens.

Yield: about 1 cup vinaigrette

LEMON PASTA

3 cups all-purpose flour
3 eggs
1 tablespoon grated lemon zest
1/2 teaspoon salt
1/3 cup freshly squeezed lemon juice
1 tablespoon olive oil
6 quarts water
2 tablespoons salt
   Butter-flavored vegetable cooking
      spray

Process flour, eggs, lemon zest, and 1/2 teaspoon salt in a large food processor until well blended. With processor running, slowly add lemon juice and oil; process until dough begins to stick together. Shape into a smooth ball; cover with plastic wrap and allow to rest 20 minutes.

If using a pasta machine, follow manufacturer's instructions to make and cook pasta.

If rolling dough by hand, divide dough into 8 equal pieces. Cover dough with a damp towel or plastic wrap to prevent drying. Working with 1 piece of dough at a time, use a rolling pin to roll dough into a 5 x 18-inch rectangle. Allow dough to dry about 5 minutes.

Beginning at 1 short edge, fold dough into thirds (dough will be a 5 x 6-inch rectangle). Beginning at one 6-inch side, cut dough into 1/4-inch-wide pieces; separate strands. Allow pasta to dry for up to 30 minutes. Place pasta in an airtight container; store in refrigerator up to 2 days. (Pasta can also be dried completely in about 6 hours on a cloth-covered rack and stored in an airtight container in a cool place up to 2 weeks.)

To serve, bring water to a boil; stir in 2 tablespoons salt. Add fresh pasta to boiling water. Return water to a boil and cook 11 to 13 minutes or until tender but firm to bite; drain. (Dried pasta may need

Spicy Tomato and Basil Salsa tops our Lemon Pasta (left) *for a heart-smart side dish. The pasta is also great teamed with rich Mustard-Caper Cream Sauce* (top). *Herbed Salmon is a flavorful, healthy entrée, and Poppy Seed Rosettes are served with piquant Cracked Pepper Butter (not shown).*

to cook longer.) Lightly spray pasta with cooking spray; gently toss. Serve immediately with Tomato and Basil Salsa or Mustard-Caper Cream Sauce (page 40).

Yield: about 8 cups cooked pasta

TOMATO AND BASIL SALSA

2 cups chopped fresh plum tomatoes, drained (about 4 tomatoes)
1/2 cup finely chopped green pepper
1/2 cup finely chopped sweet yellow pepper
1/3 cup coarsely chopped fresh basil leaves

2 tablespoons drained capers
2 teaspoons olive oil
1 teaspoon white wine vinegar
1 clove garlic, minced
3/4 teaspoon salt
1/4 teaspoon ground black pepper

In a medium bowl, combine tomatoes, green and yellow peppers, basil, capers, oil, vinegar, garlic, salt, and black pepper; stir until well blended. Cover and allow to stand at room temperature 1 hour to allow flavors to blend. Serve with Lemon Pasta.

Yield: about 2 1/2 cups salsa

39

MUSTARD-CAPER CREAM SAUCE

1¼ cups dry white wine
2 cloves garlic, minced
1 cup whipping cream
¼ cup Dijon-style mustard
¼ cup drained capers
2 teaspoons minced fresh tarragon
      leaves
¼ teaspoon salt
¼ teaspoon ground white pepper
1 container (8 ounces) sour cream

In a medium saucepan, bring wine to a boil over medium-high heat. Add garlic; boil mixture 10 minutes or until wine is reduced by half. Reduce heat to medium. Whisk in whipping cream, mustard, capers, tarragon, salt, and white pepper. Whisking frequently, cook 10 minutes or until mixture is reduced by about half. Remove from heat and fold in sour cream. Serve immediately with Lemon Pasta.

Yield: about 2 cups sauce

POPPY SEED ROSETTES

1 tablespoon sugar
1 package dry yeast
1½ cups warm water
3½ to 4 cups all-purpose flour, divided
1½ teaspoons salt
      Vegetable cooking spray
1 egg white
1 tablespoon water
      Poppy seed

In a small bowl, dissolve sugar and yeast in 1½ cups warm water. In a large bowl, combine 2 cups flour and salt. Add yeast mixture to dry ingredients; beat with an electric mixer until well blended. Add 1¼ cups flour; stir until a soft dough forms. Turn onto a lightly floured surface. Knead about 5 minutes or until dough becomes smooth and elastic, using additional flour as necessary. Place in a

Prepared with guilt-free ingredients, Chocolate Meringue Sand Traps with Creamy Orange Filling are melt-in-your-mouth marvelous! Golf Ball Truffles feature a rich mocha filling.

large bowl sprayed with cooking spray, turning once to coat top of dough. Cover and let rise in a warm place (80 to 85 degrees) about 1½ hours or until doubled in size.

Turn dough onto a lightly floured surface and punch down. Cover and allow dough to rest 10 minutes. Divide dough into 20 equal pieces. Roll each piece of dough into a 12-inch rope. Loosely tie each rope into a knot, tucking ends either into or under dough to form rosette. Place on a lightly greased baking sheet. Spray tops of rolls with cooking spray, cover, and let rise in a warm place about 1½ hours or until nearly doubled in size.

Preheat oven to 375 degrees. In a small bowl, lightly beat egg white and water.

Brush rolls with egg white mixture. Bake 8 minutes. Remove from oven and brush with egg white mixture again; sprinkle with poppy seed. Bake 16 to 18 minutes or until golden brown. Serve warm or transfer to a wire rack to cool completely.

Yield: 20 rolls

CRACKED PEPPER BUTTER

1 cup butter, softened
¾ teaspoon freshly ground black
      pepper

In a small bowl, beat butter and pepper until fluffy and well blended.

Yield: about 1 cup pepper butter

40

CHOCOLATE MERINGUE SAND TRAPS WITH CREAMY ORANGE FILLING

Make 2 recipes of meringues, as small batches yield better results.

MERINGUES

- 1/2 cup superfine granulated sugar
- 1 tablespoon cocoa
- 3 egg whites
- 1/4 teaspoon cream of tartar
- 1/4 teaspoon vanilla extract
  Pinch of salt

FILLING

- 1 package (0.3 ounces) sugar-free orange gelatin
- 1 1/4 cups boiling water
- 1/3 cup frozen orange juice concentrate, thawed
- 1 cup evaporated skimmed milk, chilled
- 1 cup reduced-calorie whipped topping

For about 8 meringues, cover a baking sheet with aluminum foil. In a small bowl, combine sugar and cocoa. In a large bowl, beat egg whites until foamy. Add cream of tartar, vanilla, and salt; beat at high speed of an electric mixer until soft peaks form. Add sugar mixture, 1 tablespoon at a time, beating about 8 minutes or until sugar dissolves and stiff peaks form.

Preheat oven to 250 degrees. Spoon meringue into a pastry bag fitted with a large open star tip. Pipe each meringue onto foil in the shape of a sand trap, about 3 inches in diameter. Fill in outline with a layer of meringue. Pipe a single layer of meringue onto outside edge of each shape to form a ridge. Bake 1 hour. Without opening oven, turn oven off and allow meringues to sit in oven 2 hours. Remove meringues from oven and peel foil from meringues. Store in an airtight container. Repeat to make about 8 more meringues.

For filling, combine gelatin, water, and juice concentrate in a medium bowl; stir until gelatin dissolves. Allow to sit at room temperature 2 to 3 hours or until gelatin starts to thicken. Add evaporated milk; beat with an electric mixer on high speed about 4 minutes or until mixture is light and fluffy. Fold in whipped topping. Spoon about 1/3 cup of filling into each meringue. Serve immediately.

Yield: about 1 1/2 dozen meringues

GOLF BALL TRUFFLES

- 4 ounces cream cheese, softened
- 1 1/2 cups sifted confectioners sugar
- 1 package (6 ounces) semisweet chocolate chips, melted
- 1 1/2 tablespoons coffee-flavored liqueur
- 10 to 12 ounces vanilla candy coating

Line 2 baking sheets with waxed paper. In a medium bowl, beat cream cheese until fluffy. Gradually add confectioners sugar; beat until well blended. Gradually add melted chocolate chips and liqueur; stir until well blended. Drop tablespoonfuls of candy mixture onto 1 prepared baking sheet; chill 30 minutes.

Shape tablespoonfuls of candy mixture into balls. Cover and freeze 2 hours.

Melt candy coating in the top of a double boiler over simmering water; remove from heat. (If candy coating begins to harden, return to heat.) Remove about 3 candies from freezer at a time. Place each candy on a fork and spoon candy coating over candy. Wipe fork after each dipping to prevent chocolate from mixing with coating. Place truffles on remaining prepared baking sheet; chill about 10 minutes or until coating hardens. Store in an airtight container in a cool place.

Yield: about 2 dozen truffles

"PAR-TEE" INVITATIONS

For each invitation (page 34), you will need plaid fabric, two 8 1/2" x 11" pieces of white card stock paper, colored pencils, black permanent felt-tip pen with fine point (optional), spray adhesive, and a 6" x 9" envelope to coordinate with fabric.

1. Apply spray adhesive to 1 side of 1 card stock paper piece. Press paper glue side down on wrong side of fabric. Trim fabric even with edges of paper.
2. For card, match short edges and fold fabric-covered paper in half with fabric side out.
3. (*Note:* To keep photocopying cost to a minimum, copy invitation design twice onto one 8 1/2" x 11" card stock paper piece, then make additional copies.) Photocopy invitation design, page 113, onto card stock paper.
4. Use colored pencils to color design. If desired, use black pen to draw over lines of design.
5. Cutting about 1/4" from design, cut out design. Use spray adhesive to glue design to center front of card.

PRO TOUR SALAD BOWL STAND

For stand (page 38), you will need a 12" dia. wooden plate, 5 golf balls, green acrylic spray paint, white paint pen, matte clear acrylic spray, and a hot glue gun and glue sticks.

1. Spray paint plate green.
2. Spacing evenly, use paint pen to write the following words several times along edge of rim on plate: "PAR," "BIRDIE," "BOGEY," and "EAGLE." Paint white dots between words. Apply 2 to 3 coats of acrylic spray to plate.
3. Position plate with bottom facing up. Spacing evenly, glue balls to bottom of plate rim.

GOLF COURSE DECOR

Our sporty links arrangements (pages 34, 35, and 43) combine traditional plaids with the splendor of lush greens — the envy of any avid golfer. For a unique buffet tablecloth, we draped a piece of plaid fabric over the tabletop and added a "green" cut from a piece of green felt. Two Tartan Table Runners (this page) crisscross the dining table.

The focal points of the arrangements are plots of real mondo or monkey grass purchased at a nursery and transplanted into green spray-painted terra-cotta saucers. To transplant the grass, line saucers with aluminum foil and transfer grass, keeping about 2" of soil attached to roots. Spray with water to keep moist. The grass is a natural bed for "out-of-bounds" golf balls and white pillar candles, which are decorated with fabric-covered poster board bands and placed in glass cylinder globes (see Steps 2 - 4 of "Hole-In-One" Bowls instructions, this page, for fabric-covered bands). For an added touch, we placed a plaid ribbon bow at the base of one candle globe.

For stands for our "golf ball" candles, we inverted small, painted terra-cotta saucers and topped them with fabric-covered poster board circles.

TARTAN TABLE RUNNERS

For each table runner (pages 34 and 35), you will need plaid fabric, 1 1/2"w plaid ribbon for trim, and 3/4"w paper-backed fusible web tape.

1. Cut a piece of fabric 3/4" larger on all sides than desired finished size of table runner (the fabric pieces for our runners measured 18 1/2" x 45 1/2").
2. Follow manufacturer's instructions to fuse web tape along each long edge on wrong side of runner. Press edges to wrong side along inner edges of tape. Unfold edges and remove paper backing. Refold edges and fuse in place. Repeat to hem short edges.
3. For trim, measure 1 short edge of runner. Cut 2 lengths of ribbon the determined measurement. Fuse web tape along each long edge on wrong side of each ribbon length. Remove paper backing. Fuse 1 ribbon length along each short edge of runner.

SMALL FLAG

RIBBON-TRIMMED PLATTER

For platter (page 43), you will need an octagonal clear glass plate (we used an approx. 10" plate), assorted plaid ribbons about same width as rim of plate, small foam brush, decoupage glue (either use purchased glue or mix 1 part craft glue with 1 part water to make glue), and a craft knife.

PUTTING GREEN

Note: To maintain trim, plate should be wiped clean with a damp cloth after use.

1. Place plate bottom side up. Measure outer edge of 1 section of plate rim; add 1/2". Cut 8 lengths of ribbon the determined measurement.
2. To decoupage plate rim, use foam brush to apply glue evenly to 1 section of rim (do not apply glue beyond edges of section). With right side of 1 ribbon length facing plate, center ribbon on rim section. Smooth ribbon in place, working from center outward and gently smoothing any wrinkles or bubbles with brush. Allow to dry. Use craft knife to trim ends of ribbon along ends of section. Repeat to cover alternating sections of rim. LARGE FLAG
3. Overlapping ends of ribbon lengths slightly onto previously decoupaged sections, repeat Step 2 to decoupage remaining sections of rim.
4. Use foam brush to apply 2 to 3 coats of glue to rim of plate to seal.

PUTTING GREEN COASTERS

For each coaster (page 43), you will need green artificial turf (available at hardware stores), green 1/16" thick crafting foam, red card stock paper and a 3 1/2" long wooden craft pick for flag, a black 3/4" dia. shank button, a white 1/4" dia. shank button, black permanent felt-tip pen with fine point, utility scissors, tracing paper, and a hot glue gun and glue sticks.

1. Trace putting green pattern onto tracing paper; cut out. Use pattern to cut shape from crafting foam. Glue shape to wrong side of turf. Use utility scissors to trim turf even with edges of crafting foam.
2. Trace small flag pattern onto tracing paper; cut out. Use pattern to cut flag from red paper. Use black pen to write "19" on flag. Glue flag to 1 end of craft pick. Glue remaining end of pick to turf.
3. Glue black button to turf at base of flag for hole. Glue white button to turf for golf ball.

"HOLE-IN-ONE" BOWLS

For each bowl (page 38), you will need a small serving bowl with rim (we used 4 3/4" dia. x 3 1/4"h bowls), plaid fabric, paper-backed fusible web, red card stock paper, poster board, 9" wooden skewer, black permanent felt-tip pen with fine point, tracing paper, and a hot glue gun and glue sticks.

1. For flag, trace large flag pattern onto tracing paper; cut out. Use pattern to cut flag from red paper. Fold short edge of flag to back along fold line (indicated by grey line on pattern). Use black pen to write either "UNDER PAR" or "OVER PAR" on flag. For flagpole, glue 1 end of skewer into fold of flag.
2. For fabric-covered band, measure around widest part of bowl below rim;

add 2". Measure height of bowl from tabletop to just below rim. Cut a strip of poster board the determined measurements.

3. Follow manufacturer's instructions to fuse web to wrong side of fabric. Cut a strip from fabric 1/2" larger on all sides than poster board strip. Remove paper backing.

4. Center poster board strip on wrong side of fabric. Fold edges of fabric over sides to back of poster board; fuse in place.

5. Glue bottom end of flagpole about 1" from 1 end on right side of band.

6. Overlapping ends, wrap band around bowl, covering bottom of flagpole; glue to secure.

FRINGED NAPKINS AND NOVELTY NAPKIN TIES

For each 17" square napkin and napkin tie (this page), you will need a 17" square of fabric, 2/3 yd of 1/2"w satin ribbon to coordinate with fabric, 6" of 1/16" dia. metallic gold cord, and a miniature golf shoe or golf bag ornament (available at specialty golf or gift shops).

1. For napkin, fringe edges of fabric square about 1/8". Fold napkin as desired.

2. For napkin tie, remove hanger from ornament. Thread cord onto ornament in place of hanger. Knot ends of cord together to form a loop. Insert napkin into loop.

3. Tie ribbon length into a bow around napkin above ornament; trim ends.

"FAIRWAY" SEAT COVERS

For each seat cover (page 35), you will need green artificial turf (available at hardware stores), two 1 yd lengths of 7/8"w plaid ribbon, permanent felt-tip pen with fine point, kraft paper, utility scissors, and a hot glue gun and glue sticks.

For playful accents, "golf ball" candles are placed on decorated stands and pillar candles are banded with plaid fabric. A serving platter decoupaged with plaid ribbon coordinates with the setting. Our "putting green" coasters are decorated with button "balls" and "holes." Golf shoe and golf bag ornaments are used to create novel ties for the fabric napkins.

1. For pattern, measure seat of chair; use a ruler and permanent pen to draw shape of seat on kraft paper. Cut out pattern. Matching side edges, fold pattern in half. Trim edges to make pattern symmetrical and to round front corners; unfold pattern.

2. Use pen to draw around pattern on wrong side of turf. Use utility scissors to cut cover from turf.

3. Place cover on chair. Use pen to mark placement of uprights of chairback on wrong side of cover.

4. For ties, fold each ribbon length in half. Glue fold of 1 ribbon length at each mark on wrong side of cover.

5. Place cover on chair and tie ribbons into bows around uprights of chairback. Trim ribbon ends.

GREAT "EGG-SPECTATION" BABY SHOWER

Bearing a banner that announces Someone's Nesting, *a little bird delivers word of this adorable baby shower! Guests and the mom-to-be will be tickled pink by the fabric-covered invitations, which feature a transferred design that's shaded with colored pencils. When friends arrive, they'll admire the lovely table, which is draped with a topper made from receiving blankets and pinned with iridescent ribbon bows and silk flowers. Taking center stage, a large papier-mâché egg is cradled in a whitewashed twig wreath "nest" that's trimmed with assorted baby accessories, baby-sock bows, baby's breath, flowers, and tiny feathered birds. The egg is crowned with greenery and flowers and has a surprise lift-off top — what a precious keepsake box or storage container for a little one's necessities! Because many of these projects are created with practical items for baby, Mom is sure to be doubly delighted with this "egg-citing" celebration.*

MENU

Raspberry-Lemon Punch

Cucumber Bites

Three-Filling Sandwich Loaves

Sugar and Spice Almonds

Minted Marshmallows

Lemon Baby Cakes

THREE-FILLING SANDWICH LOAVES

The fillings may be prepared ahead of time and chilled.

BACON AND EGG FILLING
- 4 hard-cooked eggs, coarsely chopped
- 6 slices bacon, cooked and crumbled
- 1/4 cup mayonnaise
- 1 tablespoon chopped fresh parsley
- 1/4 teaspoon salt
- 1/8 teaspoon ground white pepper

CHEESE FILLING
- 4 ounces cream cheese, softened
- 1 cup (4 ounces) shredded mild Cheddar cheese
- 1 cup (4 ounces) shredded sharp Cheddar cheese
- 1/4 cup mayonnaise
- 1 tablespoon chopped sweet red pepper
- 1 teaspoon Worcestershire sauce
- 1/8 teaspoon garlic powder

GREEN OLIVE FILLING
- 2 jars (3 ounces each) whole stuffed green olives, drained
- 3/4 cup slivered almonds
- 1/2 cup chopped celery
- 1/4 cup mayonnaise
- 2 teaspoons chopped onion

SANDWICH LOAVES
- 2 loaves (16 ounces each) unsliced white bread
- 3 packages (8 ounces each) cream cheese, softened and divided
- 3 tablespoons prepared ranch-style salad dressing
- 2 tablespoons butter or margarine, softened
- 1 1/4 teaspoons prepared mustard

For bacon and egg filling, pulse process eggs, bacon, mayonnaise, parsley, salt, and white pepper in a food processor until well blended. Spoon into a small bowl.

For cheese filling, pulse process cream cheese, Cheddar cheeses, mayonnaise, red pepper, Worcestershire sauce, and garlic powder in a food processor until well blended. Spoon into a small bowl.

For green olive filling, process olives, almonds, celery, mayonnaise, and onion in a food processor until finely chopped. Spoon into a small bowl.

For sandwich loaves, trim crust from bread so that each side is flat. Slice each loaf horizontally into 4 equal layers; place on a serving plate. For each sandwich loaf, spread half of each filling between layers of bread; top loaf with remaining slice of bread.

In a medium bowl, beat 20 ounces cream cheese until fluffy. Add salad dressing; beat until smooth. Spread cream cheese mixture over sandwich loaves. In a small bowl, beat remaining 4 ounces cream cheese, butter, and mustard until smooth. Spoon mixture into a pastry bag fitted with a small round tip. Pipe dots onto sides and ends of loaves. With a medium ribbon tip, pipe bow and ribbon streamers onto loaves. With a medium star tip, pipe shell borders around bottoms of loaves. Place loaves in an airtight container and chill at least 2 hours. To serve, cut into 3/4-inch slices.

Yield: 2 sandwich loaves, about 10 servings each

"Iced" and decorated with a savory cream cheese mixture, Three-Filling Sandwich Loaves are pretty showpieces. For each, an unsliced loaf of white bread is layered with a trio of delectable spreads. The bacon and egg portion combines hard-cooked eggs, crispy bacon, and fresh parsley, and mild and sharp Cheddar cheeses are blended into the cream cheese filling. The top layer offers a zesty green olive mixture flavored with almonds and celery.

Cucumber Bites present two delicious sour cream toppings. Fresh dill imparts its distinctive flavor to the salmon selection, and Gruyère cheese, chopped parsley, and herbs complement the other taste-pleasing appetizer. The edges of each cucumber slice are scored with a fork.

CUCUMBER BITES

SALMON TOPPING

- 1 package (3 ounces) smoked salmon, broken into small pieces
- 1/2 cup sour cream
- 1 teaspoon chopped fresh dill weed
- 1 teaspoon freshly squeezed lemon juice
- 1 teaspoon capers, finely chopped

CHEESE TOPPING

- 1/2 cup sour cream
- 1/4 cup shredded Gruyère cheese
- 2 teaspoons chopped fresh parsley
- 1/4 teaspoon dried oregano leaves
- 1/4 teaspoon dried thyme leaves
- 1/8 teaspoon garlic salt
- 3 to 4 cucumbers
  Salt and ground white pepper
  Fresh dill weed and parsley to garnish

For salmon topping, combine salmon, sour cream, dill weed, lemon juice, and capers in a small bowl; stir until well blended. Cover and chill 2 hours to allow flavors to blend.

For cheese topping, combine sour cream, cheese, parsley, oregano, thyme, and garlic salt in a small bowl. Stir with a fork until well blended. Cover and chill 2 hours to allow flavors to blend.

Score peel of cucumbers with fork tines. Cut cucumbers into 1/2-inch slices. Use a melon ball scoop to remove a small amount of cucumber from center of each slice, leaving bottom of slice intact. Lightly sprinkle slices with salt and white pepper. Place 1 teaspoon desired topping on top of each cucumber slice. Garnish salmon appetizers with dill weed and cheese appetizers with parsley. Serve immediately.

Yield: about 4 dozen appetizers

Pamper guests with these delectable treats that are wonderfully easy to make! Sugar and Spice Almonds (left) are simply baked with a sweetened cinnamon coating. For a special favor, present the almonds along with colorful jelly beans in ribbon-wrapped treat bags. Our light, fluffy Minted Marshmallows are covered with pastel sprinkles.

SUGAR AND SPICE ALMONDS

  1 egg white
  1/2 cup sugar
  1/2 teaspoon ground cinnamon
  3 cans (6 ounces each) whole
      almonds

Preheat oven to 225 degrees. In a medium bowl, beat egg white until foamy. Stir in sugar, cinnamon, and almonds, coating almonds well; spread on a greased jellyroll pan. Bake 1 hour, stirring every 15 minutes. Cool completely. Store in an airtight container.

Yield: about 4¼ cups almonds

MINTED MARSHMALLOWS

  1 cup water, divided
  2 envelopes unflavored gelatin
  2¼ cups sugar
  1 teaspoon vanilla extract
  1 teaspoon peppermint extract
      Pastel sprinkles

Line a 7 x 11-inch baking pan with aluminum foil, extending foil over ends of pan; grease foil. In a large bowl, combine 1/2 cup water and gelatin; set aside. In a heavy medium saucepan, combine remaining 1/2 cup water and sugar over medium-high heat. Stirring constantly,

bring mixture to a boil and boil 2 minutes. Whisk sugar mixture into gelatin, blending well. Chill 10 minutes. Beat at highest speed of electric mixer about 5 minutes or until mixture turns white and becomes thick like meringue. Beat in extracts. Pour mixture into prepared pan. Chill about 1 hour or until set.

Use ends of foil to lift marshmallows from pan. Use a sharp knife dipped in water to cut into 1-inch squares; roll in sprinkles. Store in an airtight container.

Yield: about 5 dozen marshmallows

Citrusy Raspberry-Lemon Punch is stirred together with pink lemonade, raspberry sherbet, and lemon-lime soda. Lemon slices and juicy raspberries adorn the fruity ice ring shown on page 44.

RASPBERRY-LEMON PUNCH

Prepare ice ring a day ahead of time.

2 cans (12 ounces each) pink lemonade concentrate, thawed and divided
6 cups water, divided
1 lemon, thinly sliced
6 whole fresh or frozen raspberries
1 half-gallon raspberry sherbet
4 cans (12 ounces each) lemon-lime soda, chilled

For ice ring, combine 1 can pink lemonade concentrate and 3 cups water in a half-gallon container. Pour 3½ cups lemonade in an 8-cup ring mold; reserve remaining lemonade. Freeze ice ring 4 hours.

Place lemon slices about 1 inch apart over frozen lemonade. Place raspberries between slices. Pour remaining 1 cup lemonade over fruit. Cover and freeze until firm.

To serve, combine remaining can lemonade concentrate and remaining 3 cups water in a half-gallon container. Pour lemonade into a punch bowl; add spoonfuls of sherbet. Dip ice mold into warm water 15 seconds. Place ice ring in punch bowl. Add lemon-lime soda; stir until blended. Serve immediately.

Yield: about 5¼ quarts punch

LEMON BABY CAKES

CAKE
½ cup butter or margarine, softened
¼ cup vegetable shortening
1¼ cups sugar
1¾ cups sifted cake flour
½ teaspoon baking powder
⅛ teaspoon salt
⅔ cup milk
1 teaspoon lemon extract
3 egg whites

GLAZE
3½ cups sifted confectioners sugar
⅓ cup light corn syrup
4½ to 5½ tablespoons water
½ teaspoon lemon extract

ICING
5 cups sifted confectioners sugar
⅓ cup plus 2 tablespoons light corn syrup
5½ to 6 tablespoons water
½ teaspoon lemon extract

ROYAL ICING
1½ cups sifted confectioners sugar
1 tablespoon meringue powder
2 tablespoons warm water
¼ teaspoon vanilla extract
Green, pink, blue, and yellow paste food colorings

Preheat oven to 350 degrees. For cake, cream butter, shortening, and sugar in a large bowl until fluffy. In a small bowl, combine cake flour, baking powder, and salt. In another small bowl, combine milk and lemon extract. Alternately add dry ingredients and milk mixture to creamed mixture. In a small bowl, beat egg whites until stiff. Fold egg whites into creamed mixture. Spread batter into a greased 9 x 13-inch baking pan. Bake 20 to 25 minutes or until a toothpick inserted in center of cake comes out clean. Cool cake in pan 10 minutes. Invert cake onto a wire rack and cool completely. Brush crumbs

Tiny and tasty, individual Lemon Baby Cakes are a sweet change from traditional shower fare. Everyone will "ooh" and "aah" over the adorable treats, which are decorated with baby booties and rattles made from royal icing.

from cake; cut sides to straighten. Cut cake into 2-inch squares.

For glaze, combine confectioners sugar, corn syrup, water, and lemon extract in a medium bowl; stir until smooth. Place a small amount of glaze on a spatula and place 1 cake square on glaze (glaze will hold cake in place). Hold spatula over bowl containing glaze. Spoon glaze over top and sides of cake. Transfer cake square to a wire rack over a jellyroll pan. Repeat with remaining cake squares. Allow glaze to harden.

For icing, combine confectioners sugar, corn syrup, water, and lemon extract in a medium bowl. Repeat glaze procedure to spoon icing over cake squares. Allow icing to harden.

For royal icing, beat confectioners sugar, meringue powder, water, and vanilla extract in a medium bowl 7 to 10 minutes or until mixture forms peaks. Divide icing into 4 small bowls; tint light green, pink, blue, and yellow. Spoon icings into pastry bags. Using small and medium round tips, pipe desired decorations onto cakes. Allow icing to harden. Loosely cover cakes until ready to serve.

Yield: about 2 dozen cakes

A charming caddy for the goody-filled favor bags, our painted twig basket is dressed up with silk flowers, greenery, a pacifier, and a baby-sock bow. Some of the same embellishments are used to fashion a keepsake corsage for the mother-to-be.

"SOMEONE'S NESTING" INVITATIONS

For each invitation (page 44), you will need a 4" x 6" piece of parchment paper, one 6¼" x 9" piece each of white card stock paper and fabric to cover card stock paper, paper-backed fusible web, medium weight fusible interfacing (if needed), three 10" lengths of assorted ¹⁄₁₆"w satin ribbons, colored pencils, black permanent felt-tip pen with fine point, craft glue, and an approx. 4¾" x 6½" envelope to coordinate with fabric.

Note: Invitations should be either hand-delivered or marked "hand cancel" if mailed.

1. Trace pattern, page 114, onto parchment paper. Use colored pencils to color design as desired. Use black pen to draw over transferred words and design.
2. (*Note:* If using a dark or print fabric that will show through parchment paper, follow manufacturer's instructions to fuse interfacing to back of parchment paper before completing Step 2.) Follow manufacturer's instructions to fuse web to wrong sides of fabric piece and parchment paper. Remove paper backing.
3. For card, fuse fabric piece to 1 side of card stock paper. With fabric side out and matching short edges, fold paper in half.
4. Cutting about ½" from design, cut design from parchment paper. Using a pressing cloth, fuse design to front of card.
5. Tie ribbon lengths together into a bow; trim ends. Glue bow to card.

"NESTING" CENTERPIECE

For centerpiece (page 45), you will need a 22" dia. twig wreath, a 12" long papier-mâché egg (our egg opens into 2 halves), 16" of wired silk flower and ivy garland to decorate egg, assorted silk flowers, silk ivy vine, dried baby's breath, 2 artificial birds, 4 baby socks, 2 pairs of baby shoes, baby bottles (we used one 5-ounce and two 9-ounce bottles), baby toys (we used 2 teething rings and 1 rattle), 4½ yds of 3½"w nylon net ribbon, 20" lengths of assorted 1/16"w to 1/8"w satin ribbons, ivory and antique white acrylic spray paint, Design Master® whitewash transparent glaze, floral wire, wire cutters, and a hot glue gun and glue sticks.

1. Lightly spray wreath with whitewash glaze.
2. Arrange silk and dried flowers and ivy on wreath as desired and glue in place.
3. For each sock bow, fold two socks in half, matching toe to top edge; stack folded socks. Tightly tie desired satin ribbon lengths into a bow around center of stacked socks; trim ends.
4. Tie desired satin ribbon lengths into bows around bottles and toys; trim ends.
5. Reserving 1 toy to decorate egg, use wire to attach toys, birds, bottles, and sock bows to wreath as desired.
6. For decorated egg, spray paint egg ivory. Lightly spray paint egg antique white.
7. Use nylon net ribbon and follow *Making a Multi-Loop Bow,* page 123, to make an approx. 15"w bow. Use wire to attach toy to bow and bow to flower and ivy garland. Glue garland to top of egg.
8. Place decorated egg in center of wreath. Arrange baby shoes on wreath as desired.

PUNCH BOWL GARLAND

For garland (page 44), you will need two 23" lengths of wired silk flower and ivy garland, dried baby's breath, 2 artificial birds, two 5-ounce baby bottles, twenty 6" to 10" long twigs (about 1/8" dia.), Design Master® whitewash transparent glaze, 20" lengths of assorted 1/16"w satin

ribbons, floral wire, wire cutters, and a hot glue gun and glue sticks.

1. Lightly spray twigs with whitewash glaze.
2. (*Note:* Follow Steps 2 - 5 for each half of garland.) Form 1 length of floral garland into a crescent shape. Glue baby's breath to garland as desired.
3. Wrap wire around center of a bundle of 5 twigs; wire twig bundle to bottom of garland at 1 end. Repeat to wire another bundle at remaining end of garland.
4. Tie desired ribbon lengths into a bow around neck of 1 bottle; trim ends. Use wire to attach bottle and 1 bird to garland.
5. Tie several single ribbon lengths into bows around garland, spacing bows evenly.
6. Place crescents around punch bowl.

FAVOR BASKET

For basket (page 52), you will need a basket (we used a 10" dia. x 4"h wicker basket), 2 baby socks, a pacifier, 2 silk flowers with stems removed, two 4½" lengths of silk ivy vine, dried baby's breath, 20" lengths of assorted 1/16"w to 1/8"w satin ribbons, Design Master® whitewash transparent glaze, and a hot glue gun and glue sticks.

1. Lightly spray basket with whitewash glaze.
2. Glue 1 ivy length, 1 silk flower, and several sprigs of baby's breath to each side of basket.
3. For sock bow, fold each sock in half, matching toe to top edge; stack folded socks. Tightly tie desired ribbon lengths into a bow around center of socks; trim ends. Use a ribbon length to tie sock bow to basket near 1 flower cluster.
4. Use desired ribbon lengths to tie pacifier to basket opposite sock bow; tie ribbon ends together into a bow and trim ends.

"EGG-CELLENT" FAVOR BAGS

For each bag (pages 49 and 52), you will need a 4" x 10" clear cellophane gift bag, desired candies and nuts, 20" lengths of assorted 1/16"w satin ribbons, 14" of 3½"w wired organdy ribbon, and liquid fray preventative.

1. Fill bottom 2" of bag with candies and nuts.
2. Apply fray preventative to ends of organdy ribbon length.
3. Matching ends, fold organdy ribbon length in half. Place bag in fold of ribbon. Tie satin ribbon lengths together into a bow around organdy ribbon and bag; trim ends.
4. Trim top of bag even with ends of organdy ribbon.

BABY SOCK CORSAGE

For corsage (page 52), you will need 2 baby socks, small silk flowers, 6" of silk ivy vine, dried baby's breath, 4 diaper pins, 20" lengths of assorted 1/16"w to 1/8"w satin ribbons, floral wire, and wire cutters.

1. Wire stems of dried and silk flowers to ivy vine, trimming flower stems as necessary.
2. For sock bow, fold each sock in half, matching toe to top edge; stack folded socks. Thread 3 diaper pins onto ribbon lengths. Keeping pins at front of bow, tightly tie ribbon lengths into a bow around center of socks; trim ends.
3. Wire back of sock bow to bottom of flowers and ivy.
4. Use remaining diaper pin to attach corsage to garment.

DRESS-UP BIRTHDAY TEA

Enchant your little princess on her birthday with a dress-up tea party complete with "grown-up" china! She can help make the fabric-covered invitations, which feature a cup and saucer motif. A pretty — and delicious — centerpiece, the Tea Party Cake is baked in bowls, assembled in the shape of a teapot, and decorated with icing and colorful candies. The decorative handle and spout are cut from a foam plate and piped with icing. On this special day of "let's pretend," decorate on a grand scale using strands of oversize baubles (they're really Christmas tree garlands!) and giant gem-encrusted vanity items. The girls will love decorating acrylic frames with "jewels" to hold instant photos of this special day. Be sure to provide a wardrobe of Mom's dresses, scarves, hats, and high heels, too, because these glamour girls just want to have fun!

MENU

TEAPOT CAKE

CAKE
1 package (18.25 ounces) white cake mix and ingredients to prepare cake

ICING
3 cups sifted confectioners sugar
6 tablespoons vegetable shortening
3 tablespoons milk
2 1/4 teaspoons clear vanilla extract
Gumdrops and assorted candies

Trace spout and handle patterns, page 114, onto white paper; cut out. Draw around patterns on a white plastic foam plate; cut out.

Preheat oven to 325 degrees. For cake, prepare mix according to package directions. Divide batter between 2 heavily greased and floured ovenproof 1 1/2-quart glass bowls. Bake 55 to 58 minutes or until a toothpick inserted in center of cake comes out clean. Cool in bowls 10 minutes. Invert onto a wire rack; cool completely.

For icing, combine confectioners sugar, shortening, milk, and clear vanilla in a small bowl; beat until smooth.

To assemble teapot cake, cut 1 slice from large end of each cake layer to level. Use a 3-inch round cookie cutter to cut out teapot lid about 1/2-inch thick from 1 cake slice; set aside. Place 1 cake layer cut side up on a serving plate. Spread 3 tablespoons icing on cut surface. Place second cake layer cut side down on icing. Use a small amount of icing to attach lid to top of cake. Reserving 1/2 cup icing for spout and handle, ice cake. Let cake stand uncovered 10 minutes to allow icing to harden slightly. Place plastic wrap over icing and gently pat with fingers to smooth icing. Push handle and spout into sides of cake. Transfer reserved icing into pastry bag fitted with a medium star tip. Pipe icing onto spout and handle in a zigzag pattern. For gumdrop hearts, flatten gumdrops and cut out with a heart-shaped aspic cutter. Decorate cake with candies.

Yield: about 12 servings

TEA PARTY SNACKS

HAM AND CHEESE SANDWICHES
4 ounces (1/2 of an 8-ounce container) soft cream cheese
1 1/2 teaspoons ranch-style dressing mix
6 slices very thin-sliced white bread, crusts removed
4 ounces thin-sliced ham
Carrot strips to garnish

In a small bowl, combine cream cheese and dressing mix until well blended. Cover and chill overnight to allow flavors to blend.

Spread cream cheese mixture on 1 side of each bread slice. Place ham slices over cream cheese mixture on half of bread slices. Top with remaining bread slices. Cut each sandwich into quarters. To garnish, use a party pick to secure a carrot strip on each sandwich.

Yield: 12 small sandwiches

PEPPERONI AND CHEESE SANDWICHES
2 tablespoons mayonnaise
2 tablespoons prepared mustard
12 slices very thin-sliced white bread
3 1/2 ounces white American cheese slices
24 slices pepperoni (about 1 ounce)
Miniature sweet pickles to garnish

In a small bowl, combine mayonnaise and mustard until well blended. Use a 2-inch biscuit cutter to cut 2 circles from each bread slice. Spread mayonnaise mixture on 1 side of each bread round. Use a 1 1/2-inch biscuit cutter to cut circles from cheese slices. Alternately layer 2 pepperoni slices and 2 cheese slices between bread rounds. To garnish, use a party pick to secure a pickle on each sandwich.

Yield: 12 small sandwiches

PEANUT BUTTER AND BANANA SANDWICHES

  6 slices cinnamon-raisin bread
  2 tablespoons smooth peanut butter
  1 banana

Use a 1¹/₂-inch biscuit cutter to cut 4 circles from each bread slice. Spread about ¹/₄ teaspoon peanut butter on 1 side of each bread round. Cut banana into ¹/₄-inch slices and place on half of bread slices. Top with remaining bread slices.

Yield: 12 small sandwiches

CHICKEN NUGGET SNACKS

  ¹/₂ cup ketchup
  ¹/₄ cup firmly packed brown sugar
  ¹/₄ cup honey
  1 tablespoon apple cider vinegar
  1 tablespoon prepared mustard
  1 package (13.5 ounces) frozen
      chicken nuggets
      Seedless grapes and pineapple
       tidbits to garnish

In a small bowl, combine ketchup, brown sugar, honey, vinegar, and mustard; stir until smooth. Set sauce aside.

Preheat oven to 425 degrees. Bake chicken nuggets on an ungreased baking sheet according to package directions. To garnish, use a party pick to secure a grape and a pineapple tidbit on each warm nugget. Serve with sauce for dipping.

Yield: about 2 dozen snacks and 1 cup sauce

Serve Cherry-Apple Punch with our tasty assortment of tiny Tea Party Snacks. The treats are made with yummy fillers like ham, cream cheese, pepperoni, and American cheese. Topped with fruit tidbits, chicken nuggets are accompanied by a tangy sweet-and-sour sauce, and peanut butter-banana sandwiches are prepared with cinnamon-raisin bread.

CHERRY-APPLE PUNCH

Make punch the day of party.

  1 cup boiling water
  1 package (3 ounces) cherry gelatin
  1 can (6 ounces) frozen pink
      lemonade concentrate, thawed
  3 cups apple juice
  2 cans (12 ounces each) cherry-
      lemon-lime soda, chilled

In a medium bowl, stir boiling water into gelatin until gelatin dissolves. In a large container, combine gelatin, lemonade concentrate, and apple juice. Cover and chill 2 hours. To serve, stir in cherry-lemon-lime soda; serve immediately.

Yield: about 7¹/₂ cups punch

PRETZEL WANDS

10 ounces vanilla candy coating
   Pink paste food coloring
1 package (10 ounces) large stick
   pretzels (about 8½ inches long)
   Pink decorating sugar
   Ribbon to decorate

Melt candy coating in a microwave-safe
2-cup measuring cup on high power
(100%) 1 to 2 minutes, stirring every
30 seconds until smooth. Tint candy
coating pink.

Dip each pretzel into candy coating to
cover half of pretzel. Sprinkle with
decorating sugar. Stand each pretzel
coated side up in a glass until candy
coating hardens. Decorate with ribbon.

Yield: about 2 dozen pretzels

MARSHMALLOW FRUIT TREATS

1 package (10.5 ounces) fruit-
   flavored miniature
   marshmallows
¼ cup butter or margarine
6 cups fruit-flavored crispy rice
   cereal

In a large Dutch oven, melt
marshmallows and butter over low heat,
stirring frequently. Remove from heat. Stir
in cereal. Use greased hands to press
cereal mixture into a greased 9 x 13-inch
baking pan. Allow mixture to cool. Cut
into 1-inch squares.

Yield: about 8 dozen treats

SHIMMERING GELATIN
DIAMONDS

2 cups boiling water
3 packages (3 ounces each)
   flavored gelatin

In a large bowl, stir boiling water into
gelatin until gelatin dissolves. Pour into an

*Add a magical touch to the day with these fanciful no-bake snacks! Pretzel
Wands* (from left) *are simply dipped in colored candy coating, sprinkled
with sugar crystals, and tied with sparkling ribbons. Marshmallow Fruit
Treats combine marshmallows with crispy rice cereal. Shimmering Gelatin
Diamonds are sure to put a twinkle in a little girl's eyes.*

8-inch square pan. Loosely cover and chill
4 hours.

To serve, dip pan in warm water
15 seconds. Follow *Cutting Diamond*
Shapes, page 124, to cut gelatin. Use a
small spatula to carefully remove gelatin
from pan.

Yield: about 2 dozen gelatin diamonds

Presented in dainty fabric-covered hatboxes as take-home favors, Tasty Necklace Cookies will remind each little girl that she's a sweetheart. The decorated cookies have two heart-shaped cutouts, one filled with melted candy and the other threaded with a length of iridescent ribbon.

TASTY NECKLACE COOKIES

COOKIES

- $\frac{1}{2}$ cup butter or margarine, softened
- 1 cup sugar
- 1 egg
- 1 teaspoon vanilla extract
- $\frac{1}{4}$ teaspoon almond extract
- 2 cups all-purpose flour
- 2 teaspoons baking powder
- $\frac{1}{2}$ teaspoon salt
  Pink and white non-pareils

CANDY

- $\frac{2}{3}$ cup sugar
- $\frac{1}{2}$ cup water
- 2 tablespoons light corn syrup
- $\frac{1}{2}$ teaspoon white vinegar
- $\frac{1}{8}$ teaspoon salt

Pink paste food coloring

Ribbon to decorate

For cookies, cream butter and sugar in a medium bowl until fluffy. Add egg and extracts; beat until smooth. In a small bowl, combine flour, baking powder, and salt. Add dry ingredients to creamed mixture; stir until a soft dough forms. Divide dough into fourths. Wrap in plastic wrap and chill 1 to 2 hours.

Preheat oven to 400 degrees. On a lightly floured surface, use a floured rolling pin to roll out one fourth of dough to $\frac{1}{8}$-inch thickness. Use a 3-inch-wide scalloped-edge heart-shaped cookie cutter to cut out cookies. Place 2 inches apart on a baking sheet lined with lightly greased foil. Use a miniature heart-shaped cookie cutter to cut out heart in center of each cookie. Use a heart-shaped aspic cutter to cut out hole in top center of each cookie for ribbon. Lightly press non-pareils into cookies. Bake 6 to 8 minutes or until edges are lightly browned. Allow cookies to cool slightly. Leaving cookies on foil, remove foil from pan; cool completely. Repeat with remaining dough.

For candy, combine sugar, water, corn syrup, vinegar, and salt in a heavy small saucepan. Stirring constantly, cook over medium heat until sugar dissolves. Using a pastry brush dipped in hot water, wash down any sugar crystals on sides of pan. Attach a candy thermometer to pan,

Continued on page 60

making sure thermometer does not touch bottom of pan. Increase heat to medium-high and bring to a boil. Cook syrup, without stirring, until it reaches soft-crack stage (approximately 270 to 290 degrees). Test about ¹/₂ teaspoon syrup in ice water. Syrup will form hard thread in ice water but will soften when removed from the water. Remove from heat; tint pink. Spoon about ¹/₂ teaspoonful candy into large cutout of each cookie. If necessary, reheat candy on low heat if it becomes too firm. Cool until candy hardens; remove cookies from foil. Store cookies in an airtight container. Thread a 24-inch length of ribbon through small heart in each cookie to make necklace.

Yield: about 3¹/₂ dozen cookies

TEACUP INVITATIONS

For each invitation (page 54), you will need a 6¹/₄" x 9" piece of white card stock paper, pink stationery paper, fabric for background, paper-backed fusible web, dark pink colored pencil, black permanent felt-tip pen with medium point, tracing paper, graphite transfer paper, spray adhesive, and a 4³/₄" x 6¹/₂" envelope to coordinate with fabric and pink paper.

1. For card, match short edges and fold card stock paper piece in half. Follow manufacturer's instructions to fuse web to wrong side of fabric. Cut a 4¹/₂" x 6¹/₄" piece from fabric. Remove paper backing. Fuse fabric to front of card.
2. Trace teacup pattern, page 114, onto tracing paper. Use transfer paper to transfer design to pink paper. Use dark pink pencil to shade teacup and saucer. Use black pen to draw over transferred lines and words. Cut out teacup.
3. Use spray adhesive to glue teacup to front of card.

Scatter these feminine pretties across the table for the girls to enjoy. Empty glass bottles are accented with acrylic jewels and wrapped in gold mesh to create elegant "perfume bottles," and a hand mirror is decorated with colorful acrylic gems for a dazzling accent. The giant tube of "lipstick" is crafted from cardboard tubes and a painted wooden egg.

TABLE DECORATIONS

DAZZLING MIRROR

For mirror (page 60), you will need a hand mirror, assorted acrylic jewels, wide tulle ribbon, and jewel glue.

1. Glue jewels along rim of mirror as desired.
2. Tie a length of ribbon into a bow around handle; trim ends. Glue jewel to bow.

GLAMOROUS PERFUME BOTTLES

For bottles (page 60), you will need assorted decorative bottles (we used empty liqueur and syrup bottles), gold mesh fabric, gold flat braid, 1 large acrylic jewel for top of each bottle, other assorted acrylic jewels to decorate bottles (optional), and jewel glue.

1. Glue a large acrylic jewel to top of each bottle. If desired, glue additional jewels to bottles to decorate.
2. To cover each bottle, gather a piece of fabric around bottle and tie at neck of bottle with a length of braid; trim ends. Trim fabric as desired.

GIANT LIPSTICK

For lipstick (page 60), you will need a 4$\frac{1}{2}$" section cut from a cardboard tube and a 1" section cut from a slightly larger diameter cardboard tube (we used a toilet paper tube and a paper towel tube), metallic gold wrapping paper, a 1$\frac{3}{4}$" long wooden egg, iridescent pink acrylic paint, small paintbrush, small plastic foam plate, craft knife and cutting mat, and a hot glue gun and glue sticks.

1. Use a pencil to draw around 1 end of long tube section twice on foam plate. Use craft knife to cut out circles. Trimming to fit as necessary, place 1 foam circle about $\frac{1}{2}$" inside 1 end (top) of tube and remaining circle just inside bottom of tube; glue to secure.

2. Cut one 4$\frac{1}{2}$" x 6" and one 1" x 6" piece from wrapping paper. Draw around 1 end of short tube section on wrong side of wrapping paper; cut out circle.
3. Wrap large paper rectangle around long tube section and small paper rectangle around short tube section; use small dots of glue to secure.
4. Matching seams of paper, place short tube section over bottom of long tube section; glue to secure. Glue wrapping paper circle to bottom of tubes.
5. Paint egg pink. Center and glue large end of egg to foam circle in top of tube.

DAINTY HATBOXES

For each hatbox (page 59), you will need a round papier-mâché box with lid (we used 4$\frac{1}{2}$" dia. x 2$\frac{1}{2}$"h boxes), fabric to cover box, grosgrain ribbon about same width as side of lid, wide tulle ribbon, a large acrylic jewel, either a Tasty Necklace Cookie (page 59) or a purchased party favor, tissue paper to coordinate with fabric, spring-type clothespins, and craft glue.

1. Remove lid from box. To cover sides of box, measure height of box; add $\frac{1}{2}$". Measure around box and add 1". Cut a fabric strip the determined measurements. Press 1 short edge of fabric strip $\frac{1}{2}$" to wrong side. Beginning with unpressed end and matching 1 long edge of strip to top edge of box, glue fabric strip around box. At bottom of box, clip edge of fabric at $\frac{1}{2}$" intervals to $\frac{1}{8}$" from bottom of box. Glue clipped edges of fabric to bottom of box.
2. To cover bottom of box, use a pencil to draw around bottom of box on wrong side of fabric. Cut out fabric circle about $\frac{1}{8}$" inside drawn circle. Center and glue fabric circle to bottom of box.

3. To cover box lid, draw around lid on wrong side of fabric. Cut out fabric circle about $\frac{1}{2}$" outside drawn circle. At $\frac{1}{2}$" intervals, clip edge of fabric to $\frac{1}{8}$" from drawn circle. Center fabric circle right side up on lid. Alternating sides and pulling fabric taut, glue clipped edges of fabric circle to side of lid. If necessary, trim edges of fabric even with bottom edge of lid.
4. For ribbon trim, measure around side of lid; add $\frac{1}{2}$". Cut a length of grosgrain ribbon the determined measurement. Overlapping ends and matching 1 edge of ribbon to top edge of lid, glue ribbon to side of lid; secure with clothespins until glue is dry.
5. Line box with tissue paper and place necklace cookie or favor in box; replace lid.
6. Tie a length of tulle ribbon into a bow around box; trim ends. Glue jewel to bow.

BEJEWELED PICTURE FRAMES

Note: These frames were designed for children to make at the party as take-home favors.

For each frame (pages 57 and 58), you will need an approx. 3$\frac{1}{2}$" square clear acrylic photograph frame, assorted acrylic jewels and costume jewelry pieces with backs removed, and jewel glue.

Glue jewels and costume jewelry pieces along edges of frame as desired.

"ZOO-PENDOUS" BIRTHDAY PARTY

For a "wild" time, carry a picnic expedition to the zoo for the birthday boy! Announce the outdoor adventure with simple-to-make invitations featuring a photocopied tiger design. Then, on the big day, give each adventurer provisions packed in a safari survival kit. Our "beastly" lunch totes are crafted using papier-mâché containers and embellished to resemble a lion, a tiger, or a giraffe. Neat take-home favors, the buckets are lined with tissue paper to cushion individually packed snacks while the explorers make their journey. A picnic table decorated with lengths of animal-print fabric makes a great "campsite" for the happy excursion. This fun-filled celebration has everything you need to ensure a roaring good time!

MENU

Rhino Root Beer

*Crunchy Crocodile Celery
and Carrot Sticks*

Gorilla Gorp

Tiger Butter Sandwiches

Paw Print Cookies

When tummies start growling, satisfy their snack-attacks with Crunchy Crocodile Celery and Carrot Sticks! The fresh veggies are served with a creamy cheese dip that's packed in resealable cups for take-along convenience. Energy-boosting Gorilla Gorp is a mix of crispy cereal and bite-size snacks. Raffia-tied cellophane bags are ideal for sharing this treat.

CRUNCHY CROCODILE CELERY AND CARROT STICKS

- 1 package (8 ounces) cream cheese, softened
- 4 ounces (¹/₂ of an 8-ounce jar) pasteurized process cheese sauce
- 3 tablespoons dried vegetable soup mix
- 32 2-inch-long carrot sticks (about 3 carrots)
- 32 2-inch-long celery sticks (about 5 ribs celery)

In a medium bowl, combine cream cheese, cheese sauce, and soup mix; beat until well blended. Cover and chill.

Yield: 8 servings, each about 3 tablespoons cheese mixture, 4 carrot sticks, and 4 celery sticks

GORILLA GORP

- 1 package (5 ounces) round cheese-flavored puffs
- 3 cups round sweetened fruit-flavored cereal
- 2 cans (1.7 ounces each) potato sticks
- 1 cup raisins
- 3 cups small pretzel twists
- 1 package (6 ounces) fish-shaped Cheddar cheese crackers

In a very large bowl, combine cheese-flavored puffs, cereal, potato sticks, raisins, pretzels, and cheese crackers. Store in an airtight container.

Yield: about 18 cups snack mix

TIGER BUTTER SANDWICHES

- 16 slices sandwich bread, crusts removed
- 3/4 cup smooth peanut butter
- 3 tablespoons honey
- 1/3 cup milk chocolate chips, melted
- 1 teaspoon vegetable shortening, melted

    Semisweet chocolate mini chips to decorate

Use a 2-inch-high numeral 8-shaped cookie cutter to cut out centers in 8 slices of bread. In a small bowl, combine peanut butter and honey until well blended. Spread about 1 heaping tablespoon peanut butter mixture on each uncut bread slice. In a small bowl, combine melted milk chocolate chips and shortening. Drizzle about 1 tablespoon melted chocolate mixture over peanut butter mixture on each bread slice. Top with cutout slices. Press mini chips in cutouts for eyes and noses. Wrap sandwiches individually.

Yield: 8 sandwiches

RHINO ROOT BEER

- 1 quart vanilla ice cream, softened
- 3 cans (12 ounces each) root beer, chilled

For each serving, spoon about 1/3 cup ice cream in an 8-ounce drink cup. Pour 1/2 cup chilled root beer over ice cream. Serve immediately.

Yield: 8 servings

PAW PRINT COOKIES

COOKIES
- 1 1/4 cups butter or margarine, softened
- 1/2 cup firmly packed brown sugar
- 3/4 teaspoon vanilla extract
- 3/4 teaspoon orange extract

The jungle is full of surprises, and one of the most delicious is our Tiger Butter Sandwiches (clockwise from left). Look closely at the "cave" on the sandwich and you'll see a tiny creature staring back at you! During the safari, thirst-quenching Rhino Root Beer is a frothy refresher. Fun, flavorful Paw Print Cookies are prepared with crispy corn flakes.

- 2 1/2 cups all-purpose flour
- 3/4 cup crushed corn flake cereal
    Small brown gourmet jelly beans
    Chocolate sprinkles

ICING
- 1 1/4 cups sifted confectioners sugar
- 2 tablespoons chocolate syrup
- 1 tablespoon milk

Preheat oven to 325 degrees. For cookies, cream butter, brown sugar, and extracts in a medium bowl until fluffy. Add flour; stir until a soft dough forms. Stir in cereal. Shape dough into 2-inch balls and place 3 inches apart on a greased baking sheet. Press into irregularly shaped 3-inch-diameter cookies. Press 4 jelly beans into each cookie for toe pads. Press chocolate sprinkles above toe pads for claws. Bake 14 to 16 minutes or until bottoms are lightly browned. Cool on pan 5 minutes. Using a large spatula, carefully transfer cookies to a wire rack to cool completely.

For icing, combine confectioners sugar, chocolate syrup, and milk; stir until smooth. Spoon icing on each cookie for paw pad. Allow icing to harden. Wrap cookies individually.

Yield: about 1 dozen cookies

When the expedition pauses for lunch, use these stamped napkins to keep things tidy. Our "wild kingdom" favor bags are fast to make, especially when you "cheetah" by fusing animal-print fabrics to plain paper sacks! The clever carriers are filled with candy and toys, then tied with raffia and decorated with animal ornaments.

"ZOO-PENDOUS" INVITATIONS

For each invitation (page 62), you will need white and orange copier paper, black card stock paper, black permanent felt-tip pen with fine point, spray adhesive, and an approx. 4³/₄" x 6¹/₂" envelope to coordinate with orange and black papers.

1. Photocopy invitation design, page 116, once onto white paper. Use black pen to write party information on photocopy.
2. (*Note:* To keep cost of photocopying to a minimum, photocopy invitation with complete party information 4 times onto one 8¹/₂" x 11" sheet of white paper

before making copies on orange paper.) Photocopy invitation onto orange paper.
3. Cutting about ¹/₈" from design, cut invitation from orange paper.
4. Use spray adhesive to glue invitation to black paper. Cutting about ¹/₈" from invitation, cut out invitation.

STAMPED PAW PRINT NAPKINS

For napkins (page 66), you will need paper napkins, a 4" square of either foam core board or wood, 1/16" thick crafting foam, non-toxic black acrylic paint, liner paintbrush, foam brush, tracing paper, graphite transfer paper, and a low-temperature hot glue gun and glue sticks.

1. For stamp, trace paw pattern onto tracing paper. Use transfer paper to transfer pattern twice onto crafting foam. Cut paw and toe pad shapes from foam.
2. Staggering paws slightly, arrange shapes on foam core board. Use hot glue to secure shapes, pressing shapes firmly into place before glue hardens.
3. (*Note:* Practice stamping technique on a piece of scrap paper before stamping napkins.) For each napkin, use foam brush to apply paint evenly to stamp. Press stamp onto napkin; carefully lift stamp. Use liner paintbrush to paint claws above toe pads.

WILD KINGDOM FAVOR BAGS

For each favor bag (page 66), you will need a small brown paper bag (our bags measure 3¹/2" x 6¹/2"), animal-print fabric to cover bag, paper-backed fusible web, several 13" lengths of natural raffia, animal ornament with hanger, favors to place in bag, and a 1/4" hole punch.

1. Follow manufacturer's instructions to fuse web to wrong side of fabric.
2. Use a pencil to draw around front of bag on paper side of fabric. Cutting along drawn lines, cut shape from fabric. Remove paper backing.
3. Fuse fabric to front of flattened bag.
4. Place favors in bag.
5. Fold top of bag 1" to back. Use hole punch to punch 2 holes close together at center of folded part of bag. Thread raffia lengths through holes and tie into a bow at front of bag; trim ends. Hang ornament on bow.

SAFARI LUNCH TOTES

For each tote (pages 62 and 63), you will need an 8" dia. x 6¹/2"h papier-mâché container (available at floral shops); 1/2 yd of 1/4" dia. natural twisted paper for handle; foam core board; black 7" dia. disposable plastic plate; acrylic paint (see color key, page 117, 118, or 119, for colors); tissue paper to line tote; small round, small flat, medium flat, and liner paintbrushes; awl; craft knife and cutting mat; tracing paper; graphite transfer paper; matte clear acrylic spray; and a hot glue gun and glue sticks.

1. For tote handle, use awl to make a hole about 1¹/2" from top edge on each side of container. Thread about 1/2" of 1 end of twisted paper length into each hole; glue to inside of container to secure.
2. (*Note:* Refer to animal pattern and color key, page 117, 118, or 119, for Steps 2 - 4.) For tote lid, trace desired animal pattern onto tracing paper. Use transfer paper to transfer black and grey lines of pattern (for basecoats) to foam core board. Use craft knife to cut shape from foam core board along outer transferred lines.
3. Use flat paintbrushes to paint basecoats on lid, including edges. For basecoat on tote and handle, use tan paint for lion, orange paint for tiger, or dark gold paint for giraffe.
4. For details on lid, use transfer paper to transfer blue lines of pattern to lid. Use liner paintbrush to paint outlines on animal (grey and blue lines on pattern), a small white dot in each eye for highlight, and either black whiskers on lion or tiger or dark brown eyebrows on giraffe. For lion's mane, use small round paintbrush to paint long dark tan brush strokes around face.
5. For tote, use medium flat paintbrush to paint either black stripes for tiger or irregular dark brown spots for giraffe on tote. For lion tote, apply dark tan paint to medium flat paintbrush and remove excess paint on a paper towel; lightly apply paint to tote as desired.
6. Apply 2 coats of acrylic spray to lid. Center and glue lid to top of plastic plate.
7. Line tote with tissue paper.

BRIDESMAIDS' LOVELY LUNCHEON

This gracious luncheon makes a wonderful gesture of appreciation to those who will attend the bride on her wedding day! Quietly sophisticated, the affair reflects romance in every detail, beginning with the lovely lace-covered invitations. Each hand-lettered announcement is adorned with a gold-trimmed card, organdy ribbon woven with golden threads, and a heart charm. The bridal party is greeted by a fairy-tale scene brought to life with poufs of tulle, clouds of wispy lace, and cascades of satin ribbons. Gracing the table, a sentimental arrangement of fresh flowers is tended by two gilded angels, which sit upon upturned crystal stemware. The rich appointments also include fine china and gold-rimmed glasses filled with delightful Frozen Strawberry Margaritas. With food as light and elegant as the spirit of the day, this tranquil repast affords an opportunity for the bride to reminisce with her closest friends. How does this occasion speak of love? Let us count the ways!

FROZEN STRAWBERRY MARGARITAS

Make 2 recipes of margaritas for nine 8-ounce servings.

- 1 package (10 ounces) frozen sweetened sliced strawberries, partially thawed
- 1 can (6 ounces) frozen limeade concentrate
- 1/2 cup tequila
- 3 ounces orange-flavored liqueur
  Ice cubes

In a blender, combine strawberries, limeade concentrate, tequila, and liqueur. Fill blender with ice. Blend mixture until smooth and desired consistency. Serve immediately.

Yield: about 4 1/2 cups margaritas

SPRINGTIME SALAD

Use pesticide-free edible flowers in salad.

APRICOT DRESSING
- 2/3 cup apricot nectar
- 1/4 cup honey
- 2 tablespoons white wine vinegar
- 2 teaspoons grated onion
- 1 teaspoon dry mustard
- 1 teaspoon paprika
- 1/2 teaspoon salt
- 1/4 teaspoon ground white pepper
- 3/4 cup vegetable oil
- 1 tablespoon poppy seed

SALAD
- 1 zucchini
- 10 cups torn assorted salad greens (we used spinach, curly endive, and butterhead lettuce)
- 1 can (17 ounces) apricot halves, drained and sliced

- 1 package (3.2 ounces) fresh enoki mushrooms
  Edible flowers, washed and patted dry (we used pansies and violas)

For apricot dressing, combine apricot nectar, honey, vinegar, onion, dry mustard, paprika, salt, and white pepper in a food processor. With processor running, slowly pour oil into feed tube. Add poppy seed; process until well blended.

For salad, thinly slice zucchini lengthwise using a vegetable peeler. Place salad greens on individual serving plates. Arrange zucchini slices, apricot slices, mushrooms, and flowers on each salad. Serve with apricot dressing.

Yield: about 10 servings

SWEETHEART CHEESE PUFFS

- 3/4 cup all-purpose flour
- 1/2 teaspoon salt
- 1/4 teaspoon ground white pepper
  Pinch of ground red pepper
- 3/4 cup milk
- 6 tablespoons butter
- 3 eggs
- 1/2 cup grated Gruyère cheese
- 1/4 cup grated Parmesan cheese

Preheat oven to 400 degrees. Line a baking sheet with parchment paper. In a small bowl, combine flour, salt, white pepper, and red pepper. In a heavy medium saucepan over high heat, bring milk and butter to a boil; immediately remove from heat. Add flour mixture all at once; stir with a wooden spoon until mixture forms a ball. Transfer mixture to a medium bowl. Add eggs, 1 at a time, beating well with an electric mixer after each addition. Stir in cheeses. Spoon

Lightly showered with a tangy apricot dressing, our Springtime Salad is as tasty as it is pretty! Edible flowers and slices of apricot are colorful additions to the bed of mixed greens. Pair the salad with savory Sweetheart Cheese Puffs, appetizing bites prepared with Gruyère and Parmesan cheeses.

batter into a pastry bag fitted with a medium star tip. To pipe each heart, pipe 2 dough strips into a slight "V" shape, using more pressure at top of heart and pulling down to form bottom of heart. (Heart should measure approximately 1³/₄ inches at widest point.) Pipe hearts 1 inch apart onto prepared pan. Bake 12 to 15 minutes or until golden brown. Serve warm.

Yield: about 6 dozen cheese puffs

Prosciutto (Italian ham), fresh parsley, and sour cream add delightful taste to the fluffy filling of Cheesy Artichoke Tarts (right). Subtly sweet, Creamy Orange Spread is a luscious complement to Quick Dill Bread, a flavorful loaf seasoned with onion and dill.

CHEESY ARTICHOKE TARTS

CRUST
- 2 cups all-purpose flour
- 1 teaspoon salt
- 3/4 cup vegetable shortening
- 4 to 6 tablespoons cold water

FILLING
- 1/3 cup thinly sliced green onions
- 1/4 cup thinly sliced celery
- 2 tablespoons butter or margarine
- 7 eggs, lightly beaten
- 1/3 cup sour cream
- 1/3 cup milk
- 3 tablespoons finely chopped fresh parsley
- 1/2 teaspoon salt
- 1/4 teaspoon ground white pepper
- 4 ounces prosciutto, chopped
- 1 can (14 ounces) artichoke hearts, drained and halved
- 1 cup (4 ounces) finely shredded Swiss cheese

Preheat oven to 450 degrees. For crust, combine flour and salt in a medium bowl. Using a pastry blender or 2 knives, cut in shortening until mixture resembles coarse meal. Sprinkle with 4 tablespoons water. Mix until a soft dough forms, adding additional water as necessary. Divide dough in half. Roll out half of dough to 1/8-inch thickness between 2 sheets of plastic wrap. Cut five 6-inch-diameter circles of dough. Transfer dough circles to 4-inch-diameter x 3/4-inch-deep tart pans. Repeat with remaining half of dough. Use a sharp knife to trim edges of dough. Place a 3-inch square of aluminum foil in each crust. Place dried beans or rice on aluminum foil to hold crust in place while baking. Transfer tart pans to a baking sheet. Bake 10 to 12 minutes or until lightly browned. Place baking sheet with pans on a wire rack; remove beans and foil.

Reduce oven temperature to 325 degrees. For filling, sauté onions and celery in butter in a small skillet over medium heat until vegetables are tender. In a large bowl, beat eggs, sour cream, milk, parsley, salt, and white pepper until well blended. Stir in onion mixture and prosciutto. Place an artichoke half in center of each crust. Sprinkle about 1¹/₂ tablespoons cheese into each crust. Pour a scant ¹/₃ cup egg mixture into each crust. Bake 30 to 35 minutes or until a knife inserted in egg mixture comes out clean. Allow tarts to stand 5 minutes in pans before serving. Serve warm.

Yield: 10 servings

QUICK DILL BREAD

    3   cups all-purpose flour
  ¹/₂   cup plus 2 tablespoons sugar
 1¹/₂   tablespoons baking powder
  ²/₃   cup butter or margarine
    1   cup milk
    4   eggs
    5   teaspoons dill seed
    2   teaspoons dried minced onion

Preheat oven to 350 degrees. Grease four 3¹/₄ x 6-inch loaf pans and line with waxed paper. In a medium bowl, combine flour, sugar, and baking powder. Using a pastry blender or 2 knives, cut in butter until mixture resembles coarse meal. In a small bowl, whisk milk, eggs, dill seed, and minced onion until well blended. Add to flour mixture; stir just until moistened. Spoon batter into prepared pans. Bake 34 to 38 minutes or until bread is golden brown and a toothpick inserted in center of bread comes out clean.

Cool bread in pans on a wire rack 10 minutes. Remove loaves from pans; serve warm or cool completely on wire rack. Serve with Creamy Orange Spread.

Yield: 4 loaves bread

Wrapped in ribbons and romance, boxes filled with Marzipan Hearts are sweet tokens of gratitude for the bride's attendants. The heart-shaped confections, created with finely ground almonds and amaretto, have a lovely marbled look. To hold the delicious favors, papier-mâché boxes are painted, embellished with elegant notions, and sealed with love.

CREAMY ORANGE SPREAD

    2   packages (3 ounces each) cream
        cheese, softened
  ¹/₄   cup butter, softened
  ¹/₄   cup orange marmalade

In a small bowl, beat cream cheese and butter until fluffy. Add orange marmalade; beat until well blended. Store in an airtight container in refrigerator. Serve with Quick Dill Bread.

Yield: about 1¹/₂ cups spread

MARZIPAN HEARTS

    3   cups sifted confectioners sugar,
        divided
 1¹/₂   cups slivered almonds
    1   egg white
    1   tablespoon amaretto
    2   teaspoons light corn syrup
    1   teaspoon orange juice
        Vegetable cooking spray
        Pink paste food coloring

Process 1¹/₂ cups confectioners sugar and almonds in a food processor until almonds are finely ground. Add egg white, amaretto, corn syrup, and orange juice; process until mixture forms a ball. Place ball of almond mixture on a hard surface lightly dusted with confectioners sugar. Knead in additional confectioners sugar as necessary until marzipan is smooth and firm enough to shape. Lightly spray 1¹/₈-inch-wide heart-shaped candy molds with cooking spray; wipe off excess spray with a paper towel. Divide marzipan in half; tint half pink. (Work with a small amount of marzipan at a time and keep remaining wrapped in plastic wrap.) Knead small portions of plain and pink marzipan together to create a marbled effect; shape into ³/₄-inch balls. Press balls into prepared candy molds, shaping into puffy hearts. Remove from molds. Store hearts in single layers between waxed paper in an airtight container in refrigerator.

Yield: about 5 dozen hearts

Our layered Cherub Cake is sure to be among the sweetest memories of this joyous luncheon. The heavenly dessert features moist apricot-flavored cake covered with creamy vanilla-almond icing. For the fanciful cake topper, a plaster angel is antiqued, highlighted with golden accents, and placed among an arrangement of fresh flowers and shimmering ribbons.

CHERUB CAKE

Use pesticide-free edible flowers to decorate cake.

CAKE

	Vegetable cooking spray
1 1/2	cups butter or margarine, softened
2 1/2	cups sugar
5	eggs, separated
1	tablespoon vanilla extract
1/2	cup apricot preserves
4 1/2	cups sifted cake flour
4 1/2	teaspoons baking powder
1	teaspoon salt
1 1/4	cups milk

ICING

1 1/2	cups vegetable shortening
3	tablespoons plus 2 teaspoons water
1	tablespoon plus 2 teaspoons light corn syrup
1	tablespoon vanilla extract
2	teaspoons almond extract
6 3/4	cups sifted confectioners sugar
	Brown paste food coloring
	Edible flowers, washed and patted dry to decorate (we used pansies and roses)

Preheat oven to 350 degrees. Spray a 6 x 2-inch, an 8 x 2-inch, and a 10 x 2-inch round cake pan with cooking spray. Line bottoms of pans with waxed paper; spray waxed paper with cooking spray. For cake, cream butter and sugar in a large bowl until fluffy. Add egg yolks and vanilla; beat until smooth. Stir in apricot preserves. In a medium bowl, combine cake flour, baking powder, and salt. Alternately add milk and dry ingredients to creamed mixture; beat until well blended. In a medium bowl, beat egg whites until stiff. Fold into batter. Pour batter into prepared pans. Bake 28 to 38 minutes, checking each pan separately until a toothpick inserted in center of each cake layer comes out clean. Cool in pans

5 minutes. Invert onto a wire rack and cool completely.

For icing, combine shortening, water, corn syrup, and extracts in a large bowl. Beat in confectioners sugar, 1 cup at a time, just until blended and smooth. Tint icing light beige. Spoon 1 cup icing into a pastry bag fitted with a medium round tip; set aside. Place 10-inch cake layer on a serving plate; ice with about 1¹/₂ cups icing. Cut cardboard cake boards same size as 8- and 6-inch cake layers. Place cake layers on boards. Ice 8-inch layer with about 1¹/₄ cups icing and 6-inch layer with about ³/₄ cup icing. Place 8- and 6-inch layers with boards on 10-inch cake layer. Pipe bead border on bottom edges of cake layers. Decorate with Cherub Cake Topper (page 77) and flowers.

Yield: about 32 servings

FLORAL ICE BOWL WITH SHERBET

Make ice bowl and freeze scoops of sherbet the day before party. Use pesticide-free edible flowers in ice bowl.

> Edible flowers and leaves, washed and patted dry (we used pansies, pansy leaves, and roses)
> 1 quart *each* lime sherbet, strawberry sherbet, and pineapple sherbet

Fill a 6-quart metal or plastic bowl half full with water. Arrange flowers to completely cover surface of water. Fill a 3¹/₂-quart plastic (not metal) bowl of similar shape with ice cubes; place in center of large bowl. Use freezer tape across both bowls to hold small bowl in place about ¹/₂ inch above large bowl. Freeze 15 to 30 minutes or until ice crystals begin to form on top. Use a wooden skewer to distribute flowers down sides of bowl; add more flowers to cover

Whether artfully arranged in bouquets or scattered along the bride's pathway, flowers lend undeniable magic to the wedding celebration. We've suspended their beauty in our Floral Ice Bowl with Sherbet, an enchanting yet easy-to-create showpiece.

top. Continue to add and reposition flowers as water freezes; freeze overnight.

Place 24 sherbet scoops in a single layer on baking sheets; cover and freeze overnight.

To serve, remove tape and ice cubes. Fill small bowl with lukewarm water; remove small bowl when it releases from

ice bowl. Turn large bowl over onto a flat surface. Place a warm towel over bowl until ice bowl releases. Place ice bowl on a paper doily or cloth napkin on a serving platter with a raised edge. Place sherbet scoops in ice bowl. Serve immediately.

Yield: 24 servings

Our exquisitely dressed table begins with a simple table drape made using lace and a queen-size sheet! Wispy bows of tulle, satin, and metallic gold ribbons are pinned to each corner. For feminine chair covers, the seats are draped with netting, then tied with lace and a matching bow.

LOVELY INVITATIONS

For each invitation (page 68), you will need a 6¹/₄" x 8" piece of pink card stock paper, an approx. 4¹/₄" x 3" gold-trimmed place card (available at stationery stores), 7" of 4³/₄"w cream-colored flat lace, ¹/₃ yd of 1⁷/₈"w pink organdy ribbon, paper-backed fusible web, an approx. 1¹/₄"w gold heart charm, black felt-tip calligraphy pen with fine point, pressing cloth, hot glue gun and glue sticks, and an approx. 4³/₄" x 6¹/₂" envelope to match card stock paper.

Note: Invitations should be either hand-delivered or marked "hand cancel" if mailed.

1. Cut a 4¹/₄" x 6¹/₄" piece from web. Matching 1 long edge of web piece to 1 short edge (bottom) of card stock paper piece, follow manufacturer's instructions to fuse web to paper. Remove paper backing.
2. With right side of lace facing up and extending bottom edge of lace about ¹/₂" beyond bottom edge of paper, center lace over web on paper. Using pressing cloth, fuse lace to paper. Trim lace even with side edges of paper.
3. For card, match short edges of paper and fold paper in half with lace side out.

4. If place card has a back, cut back from place card and discard. Use black pen to write "A Bridesmaids' Luncheon" on front of place card. Glue place card to center front of card.
5. Fold ribbon length in half and knot about 1¹/₂" from fold; trim ends. Glue charm to knot. Glue ribbon to invitation.

ROMANTIC TABLE DRAPE AND CHAIR COVERS

For table drape (page 69 and this page), you will need a pink oversize tablecloth and cream-colored lace to cover table (we used a queen-size flat sheet and 1²/₃ yds of 60"w lace to cover our 30" square table), floral wire, wire cutters, and the following items for each bow: 2³/₄ yds of wide cream-colored tulle ribbon, 1¹/₄ yds each of ³/₈"w cream-colored satin ribbon and ¹/₈"w metallic gold ribbon, and a small safety pin.

For each chair cover (this page), you will need 45"w cream-colored netting, 4³/₄"w cream-colored flat lace, 3¹/₂ yds of wide cream-colored tulle ribbon and 1¹/₈ yds each of 1¹/₂"w pink satin ribbon and 1⁷/₈"w pink organdy ribbon for bow, and a large rubber band (optional).

TABLE DRAPE

1. For table drape, place tablecloth on table and tuck edges under at floor. Center lace over tablecloth.
2. For each bow, use tulle ribbon and follow Steps 1 - 3 of *Making a Multi-Loop Bow,* page 123, to make a 6-loop bow with 5¹/₂" loops and 15" streamers. Tie satin and gold ribbons together into a bow around center of tulle bow, covering wire; trim ribbon ends.
3. Use safety pin to attach bow to table drape at edge of table (we attached 1 bow to each corner of our table).

CHAIR COVER

1. Measure from center top of chairback to desired length of cover; multiply by 2. Cut a length of netting the determined measurement.
2. Center netting over chairback. If desired, use rubber band to hold netting in place.
3. Measure around chairback; add 22". Cut a length of lace the determined measurement. With center of lace at center front of chairback, wrap lace around chairback and tightly knot at back. If necessary, remove rubber band. Adjust gathers evenly.
4. Use tulle ribbon and follow Steps 1 - 3 of *Making a Multi-Loop Bow*, page 123, to make an 8-loop bow with 6" loops and 12" streamers. To attach bow to lace on chair, tie satin and organdy ribbons together into a bow around center of tulle bow and knot of lace. Trim ribbon and lace ends.

CHERUB CAKE TOPPER

For cake topper (page 74), you will need an approx. 4"h plaster cherub (available at craft stores); a 5" dia. paper doily; a 7" square of pink fabric; 1 yd each of the following satin ribbons: $1/4$"w, $1/2$"w, and $1^1/2$"w pink and $3/8$"w and wired $7/8$"w cream-colored; two 1 yd lengths each of $1^7/8$"w pink organdy ribbon and $1/8$"w metallic gold ribbon; several of the same flowers used to decorate cake; ivory acrylic spray paint; brown waterbase stain; metallic gold acrylic paint; matte clear acrylic sealer; foam brush; small flat paintbrush; lightweight cardboard; parchment paper (used in baking); drawing compass; soft cloth; craft glue; and a hot glue gun and glue sticks.

1. For base, use compass to draw a 5" dia. circle on cardboard; cut out. Draw around circle on parchment paper and wrong side of fabric square. Cutting just inside drawn circle, cut out parchment paper circle. Cutting about $1/2$" outside drawn circle, cut out fabric circle. Clip edges of fabric circle to $1/8$" from drawn circle.
2. (*Note:* Use craft glue for Step 2.) Center cardboard circle on wrong side of fabric circle. Alternating sides and pulling fabric taut, fold clipped edges of fabric over edges of cardboard and glue to secure. Center and glue parchment paper circle to uncovered side of cardboard circle (bottom of base). Center and glue doily to top of base.
3. For cherub, spray paint cherub ivory. Use foam brush to apply stain to cherub; wipe with soft cloth to remove excess stain. Dip flat paintbrush in gold paint; remove excess paint on a paper towel until brush is almost dry. Use brush to lightly paint cherub gold.
4. Apply 2 to 3 coats of sealer to cherub.
5. Hot glue cherub to base slightly off center.
6. Tie $1^1/2$"w satin ribbon length and 1 organdy ribbon length together into a bow; trim ends. Hot glue bow to base near cherub.
7. Tie gold ribbon lengths and remaining satin ribbon lengths together into a bow; trim ends. Hot glue second bow to first bow.
8. Place topper on cake.
9. Tie remaining organdy ribbon length into a bow around stems of some of the flowers; trim ribbon ends. Place flower bunch on cake topper; arrange additional flowers on cake topper as desired. Arrange streamers and hot glue to base to secure.

ELEGANT KEEPSAKE BOXES

Depending on the type of glue used for this project, the decorations on the boxes can be either temporary or permanent. We used a repositionable glue on our lace and ribbon wrapping so the boxes can be easily rewrapped after opening.

For each box (page 73), you will need an approx. $4^1/2$" x 2" papier-mâché box with lid, 4"w cream-colored flat lace, $1^1/2$"w pink organdy ribbon, 7" of $3/8$"w cream-colored satin ribbon, pink and metallic gold acrylic spray paint, gold sealing wax and a seal stamp (available at stationery stores), either Marzipan Hearts (page 73) or a purchased gift, tissue paper to line box, repositionable glue (optional), and craft glue.

1. Remove lid from box. Spray paint lid pink and box gold.
2. Line box with tissue paper and place either heart candies or gift in box; replace lid on box.
3. Measure around width of box; add $1/2$". Cut 1 length each from lace and organdy ribbon the determined measurement.
4. Center organdy ribbon length on lace length; use craft glue to glue ends of ribbon to ends of lace.
5. Center and wrap lace and ribbon lengths around box, overlapping ends at bottom. Follow manufacturer's instructions for desired glue to glue lace and ribbon lengths to box.
6. Form satin ribbon into a loop. Use craft glue to glue ribbon loop to box lid; trim ends.
7. Following manufacturer's instructions, use sealing wax and seal stamp to apply seal to ribbon loop.

TOOL-TIME SHOWER

When it's time to assemble a shower for the groom-to-be, follow our blueprints for fun! Fabricated with heavy-duty construction paper, the handsaw invitations reveal the "tool-time" theme of this informal couples' party. Our appliquéd table runner, featuring no-sew tool motifs, lays the foundation for the hearty buffet. Specifications also call for lighthearted table accents, including a hard hat and a toolbox centerpiece that's filled with ivy and embellished with tool-shaped picks, humorous signs, and a multi-loop bow. For quick napkins, squares of fabric are simply hemmed and ringed with spray-painted hose clamps! Brand-new shop gear makes neat serving containers for mounds of Dustpan Snack Mix — zippy bites flavored with chili seasoning — and chilled carafes of Screwdriver Punch. The cocktail blends orange and cherry liqueurs into the traditional orange juice and vodka drink. With all their wonderful workshop gifts, the groom and his bride will be well-tooled for building their life together!

He came. She SAW. He conquered.

You can't PLIER away from him now!

No toolin...
It's real love!

I'm NUTS about the way
you BOLT me over!

MENU

SCREWDRIVER PUNCH

5 cups orange juice
1¼ cups triple sec (orange-flavored liqueur)
1¼ cups vodka
½ cup kirsch (cherry-flavored liqueur)
1 tablespoon grenadine syrup
5 cans (12 ounces each) lemon-lime soda, chilled
Maraschino cherries with stems to garnish

In a 1 gallon container, combine orange juice, triple sec, vodka, kirsch, and grenadine syrup. Cover and store in refrigerator.

To serve, add lemon-lime soda to punch mixture; stir until blended. Serve punch over ice. Garnish each serving with a cherry.

Yield: about 15 cups punch

DUSTPAN SNACK MIX

1 package (10.5 ounces) corn chips
1 package (10 ounces) small pretzels
1 package (7 ounces) cheese stick crackers
2 cups oyster crackers
2 packages (3 ounces each) sweet and salty peanuts
¾ cup butter or margarine, melted
1 container (6 ounces) frozen limeade concentrate, thawed
1 package (1¾ ounces) chili seasoning mix

Preheat oven to 250 degrees. In a large roasting pan, combine corn chips, pretzels, cheese crackers, oyster crackers, and peanuts. In a small bowl, combine melted butter, limeade concentrate, and chili seasoning mix; stir until well blended. Pour over snack mixture; stir

until well coated. Bake 1 hour, stirring every 15 minutes. Spread mixture on foil to cool. Store in an airtight container.

Yield: about 20 cups snack mix

SAWTOOTH CHIPS

1 can (10 ounces) refrigerated pizza crust dough
2 tablespoons butter or margarine, melted
Salt
Paprika, dried chives, and dried parsley flakes

Preheat oven to 350 degrees. On a lightly floured surface, use a floured rolling pin to roll out dough into a 12 x 18-inch rectangle. Use a large-tooth pasta cutter or pastry wheel to cut dough into 3 x 4-inch rectangles; cut each rectangle diagonally into 2 triangles. Brush with melted butter and sprinkle with salt. Transfer triangles to a greased baking sheet. Sprinkle 12 triangles with paprika, 12 with chives, and 12 with parsley. Bake 8 to 10 minutes or until edges begin to brown. Serve warm with Black Bean Dip.

Yield: 3 dozen chips

BLACK BEAN DIP

2 jalapeño peppers, seeded and coarsely chopped
2 cloves garlic, chopped
2 cans (15.5 ounces each) black beans, drained
½ teaspoon salt
½ cup sour cream
2 tablespoons freshly squeezed lime juice
Lime slice to garnish

Process peppers and garlic in a food processor until finely chopped. Add beans and salt; pulse process until beans are

Sawtooth Chips (from left) are cut from refrigerated pizza dough, brushed with melted butter, and seasoned before baking to perfection. Served in a fabric-lined utility caddy, the crisp chips are just the thing to handle our Black Bean Dip. Salsa Supreme is a fiery concoction that combines jalapeño peppers and spices in a chunky tomato base.

coarsely chopped. Transfer bean mixture to a small bowl. Stir in sour cream and lime juice. Cover and store in refrigerator.

To serve, bring bean dip to room temperature. Garnish with lime slice. Serve with Sawtooth Chips.

Yield: about 1¹/₂ cups dip

SALSA SUPREME

¹/₂ small onion, coarsely chopped
3 tablespoons fresh cilantro leaves
2 cloves garlic
1 tablespoon pickled jalapeño
    pepper slices
1 tablespoon ground cumin
1 can (14.5 ounces) diced
    tomatoes
1 can (10 ounces) diced tomatoes
    and green chiles
  Jalapeño pepper slices to garnish
  Tortilla chips to serve

Process onion, cilantro, garlic, 1 tablespoon pepper slices, and cumin in a small food processor until onion is finely chopped. Combine onion mixture, tomatoes, and tomatoes and green chiles in a heavy medium saucepan. Cook over medium-high heat until mixture comes to a boil. Reduce heat to medium-low and simmer 5 minutes. Allow mixture to cool to room temperature. Garnish with pepper slices. Serve at room temperature with tortilla chips.

Yield: about 3 cups salsa

CHEESE-STUFFED PICKLES

- 2 jars (32 ounces each) whole refrigerated kosher dill pickles, drained
- 1 tube (6 ounces) pasteurized process cheese food with jalapeño peppers, at room temperature
- 1 tube (6 ounces) pasteurized process cheese food with garlic, at room temperature
- 1 package (3 ounces) cream cheese, softened

Cut pickles in half crosswise. Use an apple corer or vegetable peeler to core pickles, leaving sides and ends intact; drain pickles. In a small bowl, beat remaining ingredients with an electric mixer until well blended. Spoon cheese mixture into a pastry bag fitted with a large round tip. Pipe mixture into pickle halves. Cover and chill 1 hour or until cheese mixture is firm.

Cut pickles into 1/2-inch slices. Chill in an airtight container until ready to serve.

Yield: about 9 dozen pickle slices

BLACK-EYED PEA SALAD

- 3 cans (15 ounces each) black-eyed peas, drained
- 1 can (14 1/2 ounces) cut green beans, drained
- 1 cup small cauliflower flowerets
- 1 small red onion, sliced and separated into rings
- 1/4 cup chopped sweet red pepper
- 1/2 cup vegetable oil
- 1/2 cup white wine vinegar
- 1 clove garlic, minced
- 1 teaspoon chili powder
- 1/2 teaspoon salt
- 1/4 teaspoon ground black pepper
  Salad greens

Cheese-Stuffed Pickles (bottom) *are cored and filled with a zippy cheese blend. White wine vinegar imparts a slight tanginess to Black-eyed Pea Salad. The chilled dish features green beans, cauliflower, red onions, and peas tossed in a spicy dressing.*

In a large bowl, combine black-eyed peas, green beans, cauliflower, onion rings, and red pepper. In a small bowl, combine oil, vinegar, garlic, chili powder, salt, and black pepper. Pour dressing over black-eyed pea mixture; toss until well coated. Cover and chill until ready to serve.

To serve, place a bed of salad greens in a serving bowl. Spoon black-eyed pea mixture over greens.

Yield: 14 to 16 servings

Keep the good times rolling with platters of big, juicy Hubcap Burgers! Stuffed with onions and cheese, these meaty manhandlers will have guests racing for the buffet. The oversize buns are quick to bake using frozen bread loaves, so you'll have lots of time to spare.

HUBCAP BURGERS

BUNS

  1 package (48 ounces) frozen
      yeast white bread dough
      (3 loaves), thawed

HAMBURGERS

  6 pounds ground beef
  1 tablespoon salt
  1 teaspoon ground black pepper
 12 slices American cheese
 3/4 cup finely chopped onion
      Vegetable cooking spray

For buns, divide each loaf into fourths. Shape each piece of dough into a ball.

Place dough balls 3 inches apart on greased baking sheets. Flatten into 4¹/₂-inch-diameter circles. Loosely cover and let rise in a warm place (80 to 85 degrees) 1¹/₂ to 2 hours or until doubled in size.

Preheat oven to 350 degrees. Bake buns 13 to 18 minutes or until golden brown. Keep warm or transfer to a wire rack to cool completely.

For hamburgers, combine meat, salt, and pepper. Divide meat into 24 pieces. Shape each piece into a very thin

6-inch-diameter patty. Place a cheese slice in center of 1 patty. Spoon about 1 tablespoon onion over cheese. Cover with second patty and press edges together to seal. Repeat with remaining patties, cheese, and onion. Transfer patties to a broiler pan sprayed with cooking spray. Place patties 4 inches from broiler. Broil 5 minutes; turn patties over and broil 3 minutes or until thoroughly cooked.

Yield: 12 hamburgers

Seasoned with chiles, cumin, and cilantro, Mexican Macaroni and Cheese brings South-of-the-Border flavor to a favorite dish. For a fun touch, we filled the pockets of a carpenter's apron with extra napkins and a "hammer."

MEXICAN MACARONI AND CHEESE

1 package (12 ounces) large elbow macaroni, cooked
1 can (16 ounces) dark red kidney beans, drained
1 can (14.5 ounces) stewed tomatoes, drained
1 can (4.5 ounces) chopped green chiles
1 can (4¹/₄ ounces) chopped ripe olives
¹/₃ cup chopped fresh cilantro
¹/₄ cup butter or margarine
¹/₃ cup finely chopped green onions (about 4 green onions)
3 tablespoons all-purpose flour

2¹/₄ cups warm milk
4 cups (16 ounces) shredded Cheddar cheese, divided
1 teaspoon ground cumin
¹/₄ teaspoon garlic salt
¹/₈ teaspoon ground red pepper

Preheat oven to 350 degrees. In a large bowl, combine cooked macaroni, kidney beans, tomatoes, green chiles, ripe olives, and cilantro. Melt butter in a large saucepan over medium heat. Sauté green onions in butter just until tender. Remove from heat. Use a slotted spoon to transfer onions to macaroni mixture. Return

butter to medium heat; whisk flour into butter until well blended and mixture begins to bubble. Stirring constantly, add warm milk; cook about 6 minutes or until smooth and slightly thickened. Remove from heat and add 3 cups cheese; stir until melted. Stir in cumin, garlic salt, and red pepper. Pour over macaroni mixture. Spoon into a greased 9 x 13-inch baking dish. Sprinkle remaining 1 cup cheese over top. Cover and bake 30 minutes. Uncover and bake 10 minutes or until mixture is bubbly.

Yield: about 14 servings

HONEY-DO BARS

- ½ cup butter or margarine, softened
- 1½ cups firmly packed brown sugar
- ⅓ cup honey
- 1 egg
- 1 teaspoon vanilla extract
- 1¾ cups all-purpose flour
- 1½ teaspoons baking powder
- ½ teaspoon baking soda
- ¼ teaspoon salt
- 1 cup chopped pecans, toasted

Preheat oven to 350 degrees. In a large bowl, cream butter and brown sugar until fluffy. Add honey, egg, and vanilla; beat until smooth. In a small bowl, combine dry ingredients. Add to creamed mixture; stir until well blended. Stir in pecans. Spread batter into a lightly greased 9 x 13-inch baking pan. Bake 28 to 30 minutes or until mixture starts to pull away from sides of pan. Cool in pan 15 minutes. Cut into 2-inch squares while warm; cool completely in pan. Store in an airtight container.

Yield: about 2 dozen bars

MOCHA-NUT BALLS

- 34 chocolate sandwich cookies
- 1½ cups coarsely ground toasted pecans
- 1 cup sifted confectioners sugar
- ⅓ cup coffee-flavored liqueur
- ¼ cup light corn syrup
- 1 tablespoon vanilla extract

Process cookies in a food processor until finely ground. In a large bowl, combine 2¾ cups cookie crumbs, pecans, and confectioners sugar. Stir in liqueur, corn syrup, and vanilla. Shape mixture into 1-inch balls; roll in remaining cookie crumbs. Store in an airtight container in refrigerator.

Yield: about 4½ dozen cookies

Present these sweets along with a list of household chores, and watch him make short work of it all! Honey-Do Bars (left) are chewy blond brownies flavored with brown sugar and honey. Rolled in chocolate cookie crumbs, Mocha-Nut Balls combine toasted pecans and coffee-flavored liqueur. A fabric-lined toolbox insert makes a unique serving dish for the tasty bites.

Construct these accessories to please the happy couple — and the rest of the crew, too! The groom's handyman cap will be a welcome alternative to a boutonniere, and his handy helper will enjoy her clever corsage, which features silk flowers and toy tools! Party favors include little candy keepers accented with ticking, paper braid, and painted nuts and bolts.

HANDSAW INVITATIONS

For each invitation (page 78), you will need a 5¼" x 7" piece of white card stock paper, red construction paper, silver acrylic spray paint, black permanent felt-tip pen with fine point, tracing paper, graphite transfer paper, serrated-cut craft scissors, craft glue, and a 4¾" x 6½" envelope to coordinate with papers.

1. For card, spray paint 1 side of card stock paper silver.
2. Matching short edges and unpainted sides, fold paper in half.
3. Trace "A TOOL-TIME SHOWER" pattern, page 120, onto tracing paper. Use transfer paper to transfer words along lower inside edge of card. Use black pen to draw over transferred words.
4. Use craft scissors to cut front lower edge of card at an angle to reveal words inside card.
5. For saw handle, trace handle pattern, page 120, onto tracing paper. Use transfer paper to transfer pattern to construction paper. Cut handle from construction paper along outer line. Use black pen to color handle "opening." Glue handle at top left corner on front of card.

TOOLBOX CENTERPIECE

For centerpiece (page 79), you will need a toolbox (we used an 8"w x 15"l x 7"h plastic toolbox), fabric for tool picks, fabric for sign picks, lightweight fusible interfacing (if needed), paper-backed fusible web, 2¼ yds each of ⅞"w craft ribbon and 2"w wired ribbon, fresh or silk ivy, white card stock paper, white poster board, floral foam to fit in toolbox, floral wire, heavy-gauge floral wire lengths for tool and sign picks, a floral pick, wire cutters, black permanent felt-tip pen with fine point, and a low-temperature hot glue gun and glue sticks.

1. Glue floral foam in bottom of open toolbox.
2. Insert ivy into foam and arrange as desired.
3. For tool picks, use tool patterns, page 121, and follow *Making Appliqués*, page 123, to make appliqués from fabric. Remove paper backing and fuse shapes to poster board. Cutting about 1/16" from edges of each shape, cut shapes from poster board. Glue 1 end of 1 heavy-gauge wire length to back of each shape. Use wire cutters to cut tool picks to desired heights. Insert picks into floral foam.
4. For sign picks, fuse web to wrong sides of card stock paper and fabric. Use black pen to write desired messages on card stock paper. Cut out messages. Remove paper backing from messages and fabric. Fuse fabric to poster board. Leaving at least 1" between messages, fuse messages to fabric-covered poster board. Cutting about 1/2" from edges of each message, cut signs from fabric-covered poster board. Glue 1 end of 1 heavy-gauge wire length to center back of each sign. Use wire cutters to cut sign picks to desired heights. Insert picks into floral foam.

5. Holding ribbons together, follow *Making a Multi-Loop Bow*, page 123, to make an approx. 8"w bow. Use wire on bow to attach bow to floral pick. Insert bow in arrangement.

TOOLIN' TABLE DECOR

For table runner (pages 78 and 79), you will need fabrics for runner, binding, and appliqués; paper-backed fusible web; lightweight fusible interfacing (if needed); and 3/4"w paper-backed fusible web tape. *For each 14" square napkin and napkin ring (page 78),* you will need a 15" fabric square, thread to match fabric, an approx. 2" dia. screw-type hose clamp (available at hardware stores), and spray paint to coordinate with fabric.

TABLE RUNNER
1. Cut a piece of fabric desired finished size of runner (our runner measures 17" x 64").
2. For binding, measure 1 long edge and 1 short edge of runner. Cut two 1 1/2"w fabric strips for each determined measurement, piecing as necessary.
3. Follow manufacturer's instructions to fuse web tape along each long edge on wrong side of 1 long fabric strip. Do not remove paper backing. Press fabric strip in half lengthwise; unfold fabric strip and remove paper backing. Insert 1 long edge of runner into fold of fabric strip; fuse in place. Using remaining fabric strips and overlapping ends, repeat to bind remaining long edge, then short edges of runner.
4. Use tool patterns, pages 120 and 121, and follow *Making Appliqués,* page 123, to make desired number of appliqués from fabric.
5. Remove paper backing and arrange appliqués on right side of runner; fuse in place.

NAPKIN AND NAPKIN RING
1. For napkin, press edges of fabric square 1/4" to wrong side; press 1/4" to wrong side again and stitch in place.
2. For napkin ring, spray paint clamp desired color.
3. Fold napkin as desired and insert into clamp.

NUTS AND BOLTS FAVORS

For each favor (page 86), you will need a small clear acrylic container (we found our 4 3/8" x 2 5/8" containers at a hardware store), fabric to cover lid, paper-backed fusible web, poster board, spray paint to coordinate with fabric, 1/4"w natural paper twist braid, 2 bolts with nuts, hot glue gun and glue sticks, and assorted candies.

1. To cover lid, follow manufacturer's instructions to fuse web to wrong side of fabric. Use a pencil to draw around container lid on fabric. Cut shape from fabric about 1/8" inside drawn lines. Remove paper backing and fuse fabric to poster board. Cut fabric shape from poster board. Glue shape to lid.
2. Glue braid along edges of lid, covering edges of fabric-covered poster board.
3. Spray paint bolts and nuts. Glue bolts and nuts to lid.
4. Place candies in container.

HANDY HELPER CORSAGE

For corsage (page 86), you will need assorted small silk flowers and leaves, 2 approx. 4 1/2" long toy tools, masking tape and desired color(s) of spray paint to paint tools (optional), a 1" long jewelry pin back, 1 1/4 yds of 1/4"w craft ribbon, floral wire, wire cutters, and a hot glue gun and glue sticks.

1. (*Note:* Use masking tape to mask off any areas of tools not to be painted.) If desired, spray paint tools.
2. Use floral wire to wire flowers and leaves and tools together as desired.
3. Follow *Making a Multi-Loop Bow*, page 123, to make bow from ribbon. Use wire to attach bow to corsage.
4. Glue pin back to back of corsage.

"GROOM" HANDYMAN CAP

For cap (page 86), you will need a sports cap, fabrics for background and letter appliqués, paper-backed fusible web, lightweight fusible interfacing (if needed), 2 approx. 2" long nails, a black permanent felt-tip pen with fine point, and a hot glue gun and glue sticks.

1. For appliqué background, follow manufacturer's instructions to fuse web to wrong side of fabric. Do not remove paper backing. Cut a 2 1/4" x 6 1/4" piece from fabric.
2. Use letter patterns, page 120, and follow *Making Appliqués*, page 123, to make appliqués to spell "GROOM" from fabric. Remove paper backing from letters. Arrange letters on background fabric; fuse in place.
3. Use black pen to outline appliquéd letters.
4. Remove paper backing from appliqué background fabric. Using a pressing cloth, center and fuse background to cap above brim.
5. Glue nails at 1 top corner of background.

QUILTERS' BLOCK PARTY

Quilters will be excited about this delightful brunch and fabric exchange. Featuring the Postage Stamp Baskets design, invitations are crafted using color photocopies of fabric quilt blocks. Fabrics are fused to poster board to fashion the spring-fresh centerpiece, which picks blossoms from the Grandmother's Flower Garden quilt pattern to fill its colorful basket. While guests mingle and swap fat quarters (quarter-yard pieces of fabric), treat them to "Basket of Oranges" Citrus Coolers, a bubbly refresher. Inspired by your clever presentations and their newly acquired fabrics, partygoers will quickly begin planning their next masterpieces. After all, there are "sew" many quilts and "sew" little time!

MENU

"BASKET OF ORANGES" CITRUS COOLER

- 1 jar (48 ounces) red grapefruit juice drink
- 1 container (12 ounces) frozen orange juice concentrate, thawed
- 1 container (6 ounces) frozen lemonade concentrate, thawed
- 1 jar (6 ounces) maraschino cherries, drained and coarsely chopped
- 1 orange, thinly sliced
- 1 lemon, thinly sliced
- 1 bottle (2 liters) lemon-lime soda, chilled

In a 1-gallon container, combine grapefruit juice, juice concentrates, and cherries. Stir until well blended; cover and chill.

To serve, add orange and lemon slices; stir in lemon-lime soda. Serve immediately.

Yield: about 12 cups cooler

"PICKLE DISH" PEACHES

- 3/4 cup sugar
- 1/4 cup apple cider vinegar
- 1 stick cinnamon
- 1 teaspoon whole allspice
- 1/2 teaspoon whole cloves
- 1 can (29 ounces) peach halves in heavy syrup

In a large microwave-safe bowl, combine sugar, vinegar, and spices. Microwave on high power (100%) 4 minutes or until sugar dissolves, stirring every 2 minutes. Add undrained peaches to spice mixture. Microwave on high power (100%) about 6 minutes or until mixture boils. Carefully pour peach mixture into a heat-resistant container with a lid; allow to cool. Store in refrigerator.

Yield: about 1 quart peaches

"DRESDEN PLATE" CREAM CHEESE SPREAD

- 2 packages (8 ounces each) cream cheese, softened
- 2 teaspoons caraway seed
- 2 teaspoons dried basil leaves
- 2 teaspoons dried dill weed
- 2 teaspoons dried chives
- 1/2 teaspoon garlic salt
  Lemon pepper
- 4 ounces (1/2 of an 8-ounce jar) pasteurized processed cheese sauce
- 3 tablespoons chopped sweet yellow pepper
- 3 tablespoons chopped green olives
- 3 tablespoons chopped green onions
- 3 tablespoons finely chopped pecans
- 3 tablespoons diced pimientos
- 3 tablespoons chopped fresh parsley
- 3 tablespoons chopped red onion
- 3 tablespoons chopped ripe olives
- 3 tablespoons sunflower kernels
  Crackers to serve

In a medium bowl, beat cream cheese until fluffy. Add caraway seed, basil, dill weed, chives, and garlic salt; beat until well blended. Spread cream cheese mixture in an ungreased 12-inch pizza pan. Cover and chill 2 hours to allow flavors to blend.

Lightly sprinkle lemon pepper over cream cheese mixture. Use a toothpick to lightly draw a 2¾-inch-diameter circle in center of cream cheese mixture. Draw 8 evenly spaced lines from circle to within 1 inch of edge of pan. Connect lines to form scallops for "Dresden Plate" design. Spoon processed cheese sauce into a pastry bag fitted with a medium round tip; pipe along lines. Fill center circle with yellow pepper and each section with 1 of the remaining toppings. Cover and chill until ready to serve. Serve with crackers.

Yield: about 3½ cups spread

Spicy "Pickle Dish" Peaches (top) *feature an aromatic blend of cinnamon, allspice, and cloves. A flavorful appetizer, "Dresden Plate" Cream Cheese Spread showcases the familiar quilt design atop a savory cheese mixture. The sections of the "plate" are outlined with piped-on cheese and filled with assorted toppings.*

Pineapple preserves lend a lightly sweet taste to Sausage "Pinwheel" Pastries. The spicy filling is baked in refrigerated pie crust cutouts.

SAUSAGE "PINWHEEL" PASTRIES

Sausage mixture may be prepared a day ahead.

- 1 pound mild pork sausage
- 1/2 cup chopped onion
- 2/3 cup pineapple preserves
- 1 tablespoon dry mustard
- 1/2 teaspoon salt
- 1/4 teaspoon ground black pepper
- 1/8 teaspoon rubbed sage
- 1 package (15 ounces) refrigerated pie crusts, at room temperature

In a large skillet, cook sausage over medium heat until it begins to brown; drain well. Add onion; cook until onion is tender and sausage is thoroughly cooked. Remove from heat. Stir in preserves, dry mustard, salt, pepper, and sage. Cover and chill 1 hour.

Preheat oven to 400 degrees. On a lightly floured surface, use a floured rolling pin to roll 1 crust into a 12-inch square. Use a pastry wheel to cut dough into sixteen 3-inch squares; place 1 inch apart on a greased baking sheet. Repeat with remaining crust. For each pinwheel, use pastry wheel to make a 1-inch-long diagonal cut from each corner. Place about 2 teaspoons sausage mixture in center of each square. Bring every other dough tip to center of square over filling, sealing tips together with water. (Pastries can be covered with plastic wrap and refrigerated until ready to bake.) Bake 9 to 11 minutes or until filling is hot and edges are lightly browned. Serve warm.

Yield: 32 pastries

"BOWL OF FRUIT" SALAD

DRESSING

- 1 package (3 ounces) cream cheese, softened
- 1/3 cup apple cider
- 1/4 cup honey
- 3 egg yolks
- 3 tablespoons apple cider vinegar
- 1/2 teaspoon ground cinnamon
- 1/8 teaspoon salt

SALAD

- 1 pear, cored and chopped
- 1 red apple, cored and chopped
- 1 green apple, cored and chopped
- 2 teaspoons freshly squeezed lemon juice
- 1 1/2 cups miniature marshmallows
- 1 cup seedless red grapes
- 1 cup seedless green grapes
- 1 cup chopped walnuts, toasted
- 1/2 cup finely sliced celery

For dressing, beat cream cheese until smooth in a medium bowl; beat in apple cider, honey, egg yolks, vinegar, cinnamon, and salt. Pour mixture into the top of a double boiler over simmering water. Whisking constantly, cook 12 to 15 minutes or until thickened. Remove from heat; cool.

For salad, combine pear and apple pieces in a large bowl. Sprinkle lemon juice over fruit and toss. Stir in marshmallows, grapes, walnuts, and celery. Pour dressing over fruit mixture; stir until well blended. Cover and chill until ready to serve.

Yield: 14 to 16 servings

A honey-sweetened cream cheese dressing embraces "Bowl of Fruit" Salad (right), *a colorful combination of fruit, celery, walnuts, and miniature marshmallows. Refreshing "Crazy Quilt" Soup is loaded with crisp veggies, including sweet yellow pepper, green onions, cucumbers, and celery. The zesty gazpacho is a delicious way to enjoy a vine-ripened harvest.*

"CRAZY QUILT" SOUP

4 cups vegetable cocktail juice
3 medium tomatoes, peeled, seeded, and finely chopped
1 medium cucumber, peeled, seeded, and finely chopped
1 medium green pepper, finely chopped
1 medium sweet yellow pepper, finely chopped

½ cup finely chopped celery
⅓ cup finely chopped green onions
2 tablespoons olive oil
2 tablespoons red wine vinegar
1 teaspoon Worcestershire sauce
1 clove garlic, minced
½ teaspoon salt
½ teaspoon ground black pepper
½ teaspoon hot pepper sauce

Cucumber slices and fresh dill weed to garnish

Combine all ingredients in a 3-quart nonmetal container. Cover and chill overnight.

To serve, stir soup; garnish each serving with cucumber slices and dill weed.

Yield: about 8 cups soup

Salad greens make a leafy bed for "Nine-Patch" Cobb Salad, which is served with a tangy vinaigrette. The namesake design is outlined with pepper strips and filled with salad toppings, including bacon, cheeses, eggs, and vegetables.

"NINE-PATCH" COBB SALAD

VINAIGRETTE
- ¹/₂ cup vegetable oil
- ¹/₄ cup white wine vinegar
- 1 tablespoon orange juice
- 1 teaspoon sugar
- ¹/₂ teaspoon salt
- ¹/₂ teaspoon dried tarragon leaves, crushed
- ¹/₈ teaspoon ground black pepper

SALAD
- 10 cups torn assorted salad greens
- ¹/₂ cup chopped radishes (about 5 radishes)
- ¹/₂ cup (2 ounces) finely shredded Cheddar cheese
- ¹/₂ small red onion, chopped
- ¹/₂ cup chopped avocado (about 1 avocado), sprinkled with 2 teaspoons freshly squeezed lemon juice
- ¹/₂ cup chopped fresh tomato (about 1 medium tomato)
- ¹/₂ cup chopped hard-cooked eggs (about 2 eggs)
- ¹/₂ cup finely shredded carrot (about 1 medium carrot)
- ¹/₂ cup (2 ounces) crumbled blue cheese
- 8 slices bacon, cooked and crumbled
- 1 green pepper, cut into 3-inch strips

For vinaigrette, combine oil, vinegar, orange juice, sugar, salt, tarragon, and black pepper in a small bowl. Stir until well blended. Cover and allow to sit at room temperature 1 hour for flavors to blend.

For salad, place salad greens in a 9 x 9 x 2-inch serving dish. Place the following ingredients on salad greens to form 9 equal squares: radishes, Cheddar cheese, onion, avocado, tomato, eggs, carrot, blue cheese, and bacon. Outline squares with green pepper strips. Serve with vinaigrette.

Yield: 12 to 14 servings

CHEESY "BUTTER AND EGGS" CASSEROLE

Assemble casserole the night before party.

> 2 tablespoons butter or margarine, softened
> 6 slices white bread, crusts removed
> 1/3 cup finely chopped green onions
> 1 tablespoon vegetable oil
> 9 eggs
> 2 1/2 cups half and half
> 2 cans (7 ounces each) mushroom pieces, drained
> 1 can (4.5 ounces) chopped green chiles, drained
> 1 1/4 teaspoons salt
> 1/8 teaspoon ground black pepper
> 2 cups (8 ounces) shredded Monterey Jack cheese, divided
> 1 1/2 cups butter-flavored cracker crumbs
>
> Sweet red pepper ring and chopped green onions to garnish

Spread butter over bread slices. Place in bottom of a greased 9 x 13-inch baking dish. In a small skillet, sauté 1/3 cup green onions in oil over medium heat until onions are tender. Beat eggs in a medium bowl. Stir onions, half and half, mushrooms, green chiles, salt, and black pepper into eggs. Stir in 1 1/2 cups cheese. Pour egg mixture over bread slices. Cover and chill overnight.

Preheat oven to 350 degrees. Sprinkle cracker crumbs over casserole in the shape of inside section of "Butter and Eggs" quilt pattern. Sprinkle remaining 1/2 cup cheese over casserole in the shape of outer sections of "Butter and Eggs" quilt pattern. Bake 45 minutes or until egg mixture is set and cracker crumbs are golden brown. Garnish with pepper ring and green onions. Serve warm.

Yield: about 12 servings

Cheesy "Butter and Eggs" Casserole layers sliced bread with a peppery mushroom, onion, and egg mixture. Before baking, shredded cheese and buttery cracker crumbs are sprinkled over the top in the shape of the popular quilt pattern.

Simple four-ingredient cookies, Shortbread "Triangle-Squares" (left) are iced to resemble basic one- and two-color quilt squares. For fun, we arranged the sweets in the "Eccentric Star" pattern. Frozen yeast bread provides a quick start to making Apricot "Sugar Loaf" Puffs, sticky buns baked with apricot preserves and chopped pecans.

APRICOT "SUGAR LOAF" PUFFS

- 2/3 cup chopped pecans
- 1 cup apricot preserves
- 1 loaf (1 pound) frozen yeast white bread dough, thawed
- 3 tablespoons butter or margarine, melted
- 1/3 cup sugar
- 1 teaspoon ground cinnamon

Grease two 8-inch round cake pans. Place half of pecans in each pan. Spoon preserves over pecans. On a lightly floured surface, use a floured rolling pin to roll out bread dough into an 8 x 12-inch rectangle. Brush dough with melted butter. In a small bowl, combine sugar and cinnamon. Sprinkle cinnamon mixture over dough. Beginning at 1 long edge, roll up dough jellyroll style. Cut dough into 1/2-inch slices. Place slices, cut side down, in pans. Cover and let rise in a warm place (80 to 85 degrees) 2½ to 3 hours or until doubled in size.

Preheat oven to 350 degrees. Bake 15 to 20 minutes or until golden brown. Invert rolls onto serving dishes. Serve warm.

Yield: about 2 dozen sweet rolls

SHORTBREAD "TRIANGLE-SQUARES"

COOKIES

- 2 cups butter, softened
- 6 tablespoons sifted confectioners sugar
- 6 tablespoons firmly packed brown sugar
- 3 cups all-purpose flour
  Vegetable cooking spray

ICING

- 4 cups sifted confectioners sugar
- 6 tablespoons milk
- 1/4 cup light corn syrup

  Violet paste food coloring

Preheat oven to 325 degrees. For cookies, cream butter and sugars in a large bowl until fluffy. Gradually add flour and stir just until blended (do not overmix). Press dough into a 10½ x 15½-inch jellyroll pan sprayed with cooking spray. Bake 28 to 30 minutes or until top is lightly browned. Cool in pan on a wire rack 10 minutes. Carefully invert shortbread onto a large cutting board. Cut warm shortbread into 2-inch squares; cool completely.

For icing, combine confectioners sugar, milk, and corn syrup in a medium bowl; stir until smooth. Pour half of icing into a second bowl; tint violet. Transfer cookies to a wire rack with waxed paper underneath. Spoon icings into separate pastry bags fitted with medium round tips. For solid-color cookies, pipe desired color icing over tops of cookies. For remaining cookies, pipe white icing on half of each cookie to form a triangle; spread to smooth. Allow icing to harden. Repeat with violet icing. Store in a single layer in an airtight container.

To serve, arrange cookies in a quilt block pattern.

Yield: about 3 dozen cookies

Piece the originals for these quilt-inspired decorations and favors using fabric and fusible web, then make color photocopies to embellish the fabric swap bags and to decoupage clear glass plates. Simple hemmed napkins are ringed with petals from Grandmother's Flower Garden, and the no-sew tray liners are a patchwork of fabric squares covered with iron-on vinyl.

BASKET BLOCK INVITATIONS

For each invitation (page 88), you will need 1 color photocopy of Basket Block (see Quilt-Block Designs instructions, page 99), a 6¼" x 9¼" piece of white card stock paper, black permanent felt-tip pen with fine point, spray adhesive, and a 4¾" x 6½" envelope to coordinate with photocopy.

1. For card, match short edges and fold paper piece in half.
2. With basket design at center, cut a 4⅜" x 6" rectangle from photocopy. Use spray adhesive to glue photocopy to front of card.
3. Use black pen to draw dashed lines about ⅛" inside edges of photocopy to resemble stitches.

DECOUPAGED PLATES

For each plate (page 97), you will need an octagonal clear glass plate (we used an approx. 10½" plate), 1 color photocopy of Basket Block (see Quilt-Block Designs instructions, page 99), a white paper doily slightly smaller than plate, tracing paper, foam brush, matte clear acrylic spray, and decoupage glue (either use purchased glue or mix 1 part craft glue with 1 part water to make glue).

Note: To maintain design, plates should be wiped clean with a damp cloth after use.

1. For pattern, place plate bottom side up. Trace shape of center of plate onto tracing paper; cut out. Center pattern on photocopy. Use a pencil to lightly draw around pattern. Cut out shape along drawn lines.
2. To decoupage plate, use foam brush to apply glue evenly to center bottom of plate. With right side of photocopy facing plate, place photocopy on plate and

smooth in place, working from center outward and gently smoothing any wrinkles or bubbles in photocopy with brush.
3. Centering doily on plate, repeat Step 2 to decoupage doily onto bottom of plate. Use a damp paper towel to gently wipe off any excess glue around edges of doily.
4. Apply 2 to 3 coats of acrylic spray to bottom of plate.

FABRIC SWAP BAGS

For each bag (page 97), you will need 1 color photocopy of Basket Block (see Quilt-Block Designs instructions, page 99), an approx. 10½" x 13" paper gift bag with handles, two ¾" x 10½" fabric strips cut with pinking shears for trim, ¾"w paper-backed fusible web tape, black permanent felt-tip pen with fine point, tracing paper, graphite transfer paper, and spray adhesive.

1. With basket design at center, cut a 4⅜" x 6" rectangle from photocopy. Use spray adhesive to glue photocopy at center of bag.
2. Trace "SO MANY QUILTS" and "SO LITTLE TIME" patterns, page 115, onto tracing paper. Use transfer paper to transfer "SO MANY QUILTS" onto bag about ¼" above photocopy and "SO LITTLE TIME" about ¼" below photocopy. Use black pen to draw over transferred lines and to draw dashed lines about ⅛" outside edges of photocopy to resemble stitches.
3. Follow manufacturer's instructions to fuse web tape to wrong sides of trim strips; remove paper backing. Using a pressing cloth, fuse 1 trim strip to bag about 1" from top edge and remaining strip about ¾" from bottom edge of bag.

NAPKINS AND FLOWER GARDEN NAPKIN RINGS

For each 18" square napkin (page 97), you will need a 19" fabric square and thread to match fabric.
For each napkin ring (page 97), you will need 1 color photocopy of Flower Garden Block (see Quilt-Block Designs instructions, page 99), poster board, 2 silk leaves, 7" of ⅝"w craft ribbon, spray adhesive, and a hot glue gun and glue sticks.

NAPKIN
Press edges of fabric square ¼" to wrong side; press ¼" to wrong side again and stitch in place.

NAPKIN RING
1. Overlap ends of ribbon length about ½" to form a loop; hot glue to secure.
2. Use spray adhesive to glue photocopy to poster board. Cut block from poster board.
3. Hot glue stems of leaves to back of block.
4. Hot glue block to ribbon loop, covering ends.
5. Fold napkin as desired and insert into napkin ring.

FLOWER BASKET CENTERPIECE

Note: If making both napkin rings and centerpiece, make napkin rings first.

For centerpiece (page 89), you will need 3 fabric Flower Garden Blocks from Quilt-Block Designs instructions, page 99 (after blocks are photocopied for napkin rings, cut blocks from poster board to use in centerpiece); fabrics for basket; paper-backed fusible web; lightweight fusible interfacing (if needed); poster board; 3 approx. 8" long stems with leaves cut from silk flowers; tracing paper; two

8-ounce plastic foam cups; and a low-temperature hot glue gun and glue sticks.

1. (*Note:* To fuse a lightweight fabric over a dark or print fabric, follow manufacturer's instructions to fuse interfacing to wrong side of fabric before fusing web to fabric.) For basket, follow manufacturer's instructions to fuse web to wrong sides of fabrics.

2. For handle pattern, use pattern, page 115, and follow *Tracing Patterns,* page 123. Use handle pattern to cut handle from fabric.

3. For basket, cut a 7¹/₂" square of fabric; cut square in half diagonally and discard 1 half. For basket base, repeat, cutting a triangle from a 4³/₄" fabric square.

4. Remove paper backing from shapes. Fuse handle to poster board. Overlapping basket triangle over base triangle, fuse shapes to poster board. Cut handle and basket from poster board.

5. With handle extending about 6¹/₂" above top of basket, glue ends of handle to top back of basket.

6. Stack foam cups upside down. Glue cups to bottom center back of basket (Fig. 1).

Fig. 1

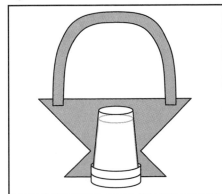

7. Glue 1 Flower Garden Block to each flower stem. Insert stems into foam cups. If necessary, glue to secure.

QUILT-BLOCK DESIGNS

Note: Some of the projects in this section are made using color photocopies of the following fused quilt-block designs. For each project, take quilt-block design to a copy center to have color photocopies made.

BASKET BLOCK
You will need an 8¹/₂" fabric square for background, 8 coordinating fabrics for appliqués, paper-backed fusible web, lightweight fusible interfacing (if needed), and poster board.

1. (*Note:* Only a 4³/₈" x 6" portion of design is used for each invitation and swap bag. To keep photocopying cost to a minimum, copy this portion of design twice on an 8¹/₂" x 11" sheet of paper, then make additional photocopies for those projects.) Follow manufacturer's instructions to fuse web to wrong side of background fabric square; remove paper backing. Fuse fabric square to poster board; cut square from poster board.

2. Use basket block patterns, page 115, and follow *Making Appliqués*, page 123, to make 4 appliqués from each pattern.

3. Remove paper backing from appliqués and arrange at center of background; fuse in place.

FLOWER GARDEN BLOCK
You will need 7 coordinating fabrics for appliqués, paper-backed fusible web, and an 8¹/₂" x 11" piece of poster board.

1. (*Note:* To keep photocopying cost to a minimum, follow Steps 1 and 2 to make 6 blocks to fill poster board piece; position blocks about ¹/₂" apart for ease in cutting.) Use flower garden pattern, page 115, and follow *Making Appliqués*, page 123, to make 1 appliqué from each fabric.

2. Remove paper backing from appliqués and arrange on poster board piece with sides touching to form Flower Garden Block; fuse in place.

PATCHWORK LAP TRAY LINERS

For each liner to fit an approx. 13" x 19" tray (page 97), you will need a 10¹/₂" x 16" fabric piece for background, assorted fabrics for patchwork borders and trim, paper-backed fusible web, lightweight fusible interfacing (if needed), and Therm O Web HeatnBond® Iron-On Flexible Vinyl (we used 17"w vinyl; available at fabric stores).

1. (*Note:* To fuse a lightweight fabric over a dark or print fabric, follow manufacturer's instructions to fuse interfacing to wrong side of fabric before fusing web to fabric.) Follow manufacturer's instructions to fuse web to wrong sides of border and trim fabrics. Remove paper backing.

2. For borders, cut thirteen 2¹/₄" squares from border fabrics. Overlapping and trimming squares as desired, arrange squares along short edges of background fabric piece; fuse in place.

3. For trim, cut four ³/₈" x 10¹/₂" and two ³/₈" x 16" strips from trim fabric. Place trim strips along inner edges of borders and outer edges of liner; fuse in place.

4. Place liner right side up on a protected ironing board. Follow manufacturer's instructions to fuse vinyl to liner. Trim vinyl even with edges of liner.

MIDNIGHT PROM BUFFET

The excitement of prom night doesn't have to end when the dance is over! This midnight buffet is a wonderful continuation of the evening for a special group of seniors. Announce the event with fun party hat invitations that are embellished with paper ruffles and dots of paint. The glitzy centerpiece is simple to create by arranging balloons and party favors in a colorful gift bag. Adding to the air of celebration, cellophane-wrapped bottles are tied with curling ribbon and filled with noisemakers, party hat picks, and shiny star garlands. Multicolored lights, streamers, and bright fabrics are combined with these glittering accents to enhance the spirit of revelry. Served in jeweled party goblets, Sparkling Fruit Tea will encourage many good-luck toasts — and the fun glasses make great mementos of the event! All during the party, take lots of snapshots with an instant camera and surprise each guest with a personal memory album featuring one of the photographs. What "fun-tastic" souvenirs for this unforgettable night!

MENU

SPARKLING FRUIT TEA

  4 cups water
 15 orange and spice-flavored tea bags
  1 cup sugar
  1 can (12 ounces) frozen apple juice concentrate, thawed
4 1/2 cups cold water
  1 bottle (750 ml) sparkling white grape juice, chilled

In a large saucepan, bring 4 cups water to a boil. Remove from heat; add tea bags. Cover and steep 10 minutes; remove tea bags. Add sugar; stir until dissolved. In a 1-gallon container, combine apple juice concentrate and cold water. Stir in tea mixture. Cover and chill.

To serve, add grape juice to tea mixture. Serve immediately.

Yield: about 13 cups fruit tea

CHEESY BEAN BURRITOS

  3 cans (16 ounces each) refried beans
  2 cups (8 ounces) shredded Monterey Jack cheese with jalapeño peppers
  1 can (4.5 ounces) chopped green chiles
 20 slices (about 16 ounces) half-moon-shaped Monterey Jack cheese with jalapeño peppers
  2 packages (10 count each) 7-inch flour tortillas
    Salsa to serve

Preheat oven to 325 degrees. In a large bowl, combine beans, shredded cheese, and green chiles. For each burrito, place 1 cheese slice on a tortilla, matching round edges. Spread about 1/4 cup bean mixture over cheese. Beginning with cheese side, roll up tortilla. Place burritos, seam side down, in 2 lightly greased 9 x 13-inch baking pans. Cover with aluminum foil. Bake 40 to 45 minutes or until burritos are heated through and cheese melts. Serve warm with salsa.

Yield: 20 burritos

EASY RANCH-STYLE POTATOES

  1 package (5 pounds) frozen potato nuggets
1/2 cup vegetable oil
  3 packages (0.4 ounces each) ranch-style salad dressing mix

Preheat oven to 450 degrees. Place a single layer of potatoes in 2 ungreased jellyroll pans. In a small bowl, combine oil and dressing mix; stir until well blended. Drizzle over potatoes. Bake 30 to 35 minutes or until potatoes are golden brown and crisp, stirring every 10 minutes. Serve warm.

Yield: about 20 servings

SAUCY SAUSAGES

  1 jar (18 ounces) red plum jam
1/4 cup prepared mustard
  1 package (16 ounces) smoked cocktail sausages

In a large saucepan over medium-low heat, combine jam and mustard; stir until smooth. Add sausages; stirring occasionally, cook 10 to 15 minutes or until heated through. Serve warm.

Yield: about 4 dozen sausages

After an evening of dancing, teens will appreciate these energy-boosting choices! Pepper Jack cheese and green chiles add spice to Cheesy Bean Burritos (clockwise from left). Big on taste, Easy Ranch-Style Potatoes are tasty morsels that have been drizzled with flavored oil and baked. A mixture of red plum jam and mustard gives Saucy Sausages their sweet-and-sour appeal.

CHEESE AND BACON WAFFLES

1³/₄ cups milk
  3 eggs, separated
 ¹/₄ cup butter or margarine, melted
  2 cups all-purpose flour
  3 teaspoons baking powder
 ¹/₂ teaspoon salt
  1 cup (4 ounces) finely shredded
     sharp Cheddar cheese
  8 slices bacon, cooked and
     crumbled

Preheat an 8-inch-square waffle iron.
In a large bowl, combine milk, egg yolks,
and butter; beat until smooth. In a small
bowl, combine flour, baking powder, and
salt. Add dry ingredients and cheese to
milk mixture and blend; do not overmix.
In another small bowl, beat egg whites
until stiff. Fold egg whites and bacon into
batter. For each waffle, pour 1 to 1¹/₄ cups
batter onto center of waffle iron. Bake 5 to
8 minutes or according to manufacturer's
instructions. Serve warm with Maple
Butter.

Yield: about sixteen 4-inch waffles

MAPLE BUTTER

¹/₂ cup butter or margarine, softened
¹/₄ cup maple syrup

In a small bowl, beat butter and maple
syrup until blended. Transfer to a serving
dish. Cover and chill.

Serve at room temperature with Cheese
and Bacon Waffles.

Yield: about ³/₄ cup maple butter

*Cheese and Bacon Waffles are in a class of their own! Prepared with
sharp Cheddar cheese and crisp bacon, the warm, fluffy waffles are delicious
alone, but they're even more mouth-watering when topped with creamy
Maple Butter.*

FRUIT TRIFLE WITH HONEY-YOGURT DRESSING

2 cans (15¼ ounces each)
     pineapple rings in juice
3 containers (8 ounces each)
     lemon yogurt
½ cup honey
3 navel oranges, peeled, sliced
     into rings, and divided
3 small grapefruit, peeled, sliced
     into rings, and divided
5 kiwi fruit, peeled, sliced, and
     divided
1 pound seedless red grapes,
     divided
1 pound seedless green grapes,
     divided
2 cups miniature marshmallows,
     divided
     Lemon slices to garnish

Drain pineapple rings, reserving juice;
set rings aside. In a medium bowl,
combine yogurt, honey, and ⅓ cup
reserved pineapple juice; cover and chill.

In a 4-quart trifle bowl, layer half of
each of the following: orange slices,
grapefruit slices, kiwi fruit slices,
pineapple rings, red grapes, green grapes,
and marshmallows. Repeat layers with
remaining fruit and marshmallows. Cover
and chill until ready to serve. Garnish
honey-yogurt dressing with lemon slices
and serve with fruit salad.

Yield: about 16 cups fruit salad and about
3¼ cups dressing

CRISPY APPLE SQUARES

1 can (21 ounces) apple pie filling
½ cup sugar
1½ teaspoons ground cinnamon
1 package (12 ounces) wonton
     wrappers
     Vegetable oil

Our colorful Fruit Trifle with Honey-Yogurt Dressing (top) is an easy-to-make treat. Featuring layers of fresh fruit tidbits and marshmallows, it's a light alternative to rich sweets. Crispy Apple Squares are miniature delights! The fruit-filled pockets are prepared using wonton wrappers and coated with cinnamon and sugar.

Process pie filling in a food processor
until coarsely chopped. In a medium bowl
or a large plastic bag, combine sugar and
cinnamon; set aside. For each apple
square, place 1 wonton wrapper on a flat
surface. Spoon 1 rounded teaspoonful
apple pie filling into center of wrapper.
Moisten points of wrapper with water.
Fold 2 opposite points over filling; press to
seal. Fold 2 remaining points over filling;
press to seal. Place squares, sealed side
down, on a baking sheet. (Filled squares
can be covered with plastic wrap and
chilled until ready to fry.) Heat oil in a
deep-fat fryer or deep skillet. With sealed
side down, place a single layer of squares
in hot oil. Fry, turning once, until filling is
heated through and wrapper is golden
brown. Drain on paper towels. Toss hot
squares in sugar mixture until well coated.
Serve warm.

Yield: about 4 dozen apple squares

TROPICAL GRANOLA SNACK MIX

- 4 cups graham cereal squares
- 4 cups round toasted oat cereal
- 1 package (6 ounces) dried pineapple chunks (about 1¼ cups)
- 1 package (5 ounces) dried banana chips (about 1½ cups)
- 1 cup dried coconut chips
- 1 cup sunflower kernels
- 1 cup golden raisins
- ¾ cup slivered almonds
- ¾ cup firmly packed brown sugar
- ⅓ cup vegetable oil
- 6 tablespoons frozen orange juice concentrate, thawed
- 3 tablespoons honey

Preheat oven to 300 degrees. In a large roasting pan, combine cereals, pineapple chunks, banana chips, coconut chips, sunflower kernels, raisins, and almonds. In a small bowl, combine brown sugar, oil, juice concentrate, and honey; stir until well blended. Pour over cereal mixture; stir until well coated. Stirring every 10 minutes, bake 40 to 45 minutes or until lightly browned (mixture will be slightly moist). Spread on waxed paper and allow to cool. Store in an airtight container in a cool place.

Yield: about 14 cups snack mix

CINNAMON CANDY CORN

- 6 quarts popped white popcorn
- 1¾ cups sugar
- 1 cup butter or margarine
- ½ cup light corn syrup
- ½ teaspoon salt
- 3 cups miniature marshmallows
- ¼ teaspoon cinnamon-flavored oil
- ¼ teaspoon red liquid food coloring

Preheat oven to 250 degrees. Place popcorn in a greased large roasting pan.

Instead of the usual chips and dips, tempt partygoers with our crunchy Tropical Granola Snack Mix (left). Sweet, flavorful Cinnamon Candy Corn is sure to be a hit. To preserve the magic of the night, make a fabric-covered autograph book for each guest to keep. A photo frame on the front will showcase a special party picture snapped with your instant camera!

In a large saucepan, combine sugar, butter, corn syrup, and salt. Stirring constantly, cook over medium heat 8 to 10 minutes or until mixture boils. Boil 2 minutes without stirring. Remove from heat; add marshmallows. Stir until marshmallows melt. Stir in cinnamon oil and food coloring. Pour syrup over popcorn, stirring until well coated. Bake 1 hour, stirring every 15 minutes. Spread on lightly greased aluminum foil to cool. Store in an airtight container.

Yield: about 25 cups candy corn

CHERRY COCOA MIX

6¼ cups nonfat dry milk powder

1 jar (16 ounces) non-dairy powdered creamer

1 package (16 ounces) chocolate mix for milk

1 package (16 ounces) confectioners sugar

½ cup cocoa

2 packages (0.13 ounces each) unsweetened cherry-flavored soft drink mix

Whipped cream and maraschino cherries with stems to garnish

In a very large bowl, combine dry milk, creamer, chocolate mix, confectioners sugar, cocoa, and soft drink mix. To serve, combine 2½ heaping tablespoons cocoa mix with 6 ounces hot water. Garnish each serving with whipped cream and a cherry.

Yield: about 15 cups cocoa mix

CONFETTI CANDY

2 cups sugar

1 cup light corn syrup

½ cup water

¼ teaspoon cotton candy-flavored oil

7 teaspoons assorted colors of coarse decorating sugars (we used red, green, yellow, orange, pink, blue, and purple)

Lightly grease a 10½ x 15½-inch jellyroll pan. Butter sides of a heavy 3-quart saucepan. Combine sugar, corn syrup, and water in pan. Stirring constantly, cook over medium-low heat until sugar dissolves. Using a pastry brush dipped in hot water, wash down any sugar crystals on sides of pan. Attach a candy thermometer to pan, making sure thermometer does not touch bottom of pan. Increase heat to medium-high and bring to a boil. Cook, without stirring,

Offer mugs of warming Cherry Cocoa to chase away the late-night chill. A sprinkling of colorful sugar gives Confetti Candy added sparkle!

until syrup reaches hard-crack stage (approximately 300 to 310 degrees). Test about ½ teaspoon syrup in ice water. Syrup will form brittle threads in ice water and will remain brittle when removed from the water. Remove from heat and stir in cotton candy oil. Immediately pour into prepared pan. Quickly sprinkle decorating sugars over candy. Allow candy to cool completely; break into pieces. Store in an airtight container.

Yield: about 1¼ pounds candy

4. Use black pen to write "Party!" several times on hat.

5. Use end of paintbrush handle dipped in paint to paint dots on hat as desired.

6. For pom-pom, use compass to draw a 1" dia. circle on 1 side (back) of 2" paper square. Use craft scissors to cut out circle.

7. For trim along bottom edge of hat, use craft scissors to cut an approx. 3/4" x 15" strip of tissue paper.

8. Center and glue hat to front of card. Glue pom-pom to top of hat. Glue trim along bottom edge of hat, pleating paper to form ruffle. If necessary, trim ruffle ends even with sides of card.

PARTY WREATH

To make our festive wreath (this page), we spray painted an 18" diameter grapevine wreath white and wrapped it with an assortment of curling ribbons, leaving ample ribbon ends for curling. We added a multi-loop bow made from several ribbon lengths on 1 side (see *Making a Multi-Loop Bow*, page 123).

Next, we hot glued sprays of metallic shooting stars and 2 party hats to the wreath (for each party hat, follow Party Hat Invitations instructions, this page, cutting card from an unfolded piece of card stock paper and omitting Step 4). We also attached 2 bright balloons on sticks (available at party supply stores) to the wreath.

To make a definite party statement, we traced star pattern, page 122, onto tracing paper and cut it out, then used the pattern to cut star from card stock paper. We decorated the star with dots of acrylic paint applied using the end of a paintbrush handle and, for a final touch, added a boldly printed message using a black marker. We hot glued the star to the wreath.

Wow revelers with this bright balloon wreath and let the party spirit start at the door! The painted grapevine wreath is festooned with an array of shimmering ribbons, metallic star sprays, a multi-loop bow, paper party hats, and a star cutout.

PARTY HAT INVITATIONS

For each invitation (page 100), you will need the following pieces of card stock paper in assorted colors: 7" x 10" for card, 6" x 7" for hat, and a 2" square for pom-pom; tissue paper for trim; acrylic paint and small paintbrush for dots on hat; black permanent felt-tip pen with fine point; serrated-cut craft scissors; drawing compass; tracing paper; craft glue; and an approx. 4 3/4" x 6 1/2" envelope to coordinate with card stock papers.

1. Trace card pattern, page 122, onto tracing paper; cut out.

2. For card, match short edges and fold 7" x 10" paper piece in half. Place pattern on fold of paper as indicated and use a pencil to draw around pattern. Cutting through both layers of paper, cut out card along drawn lines.

3. For hat, draw around card pattern on 6" x 7" paper piece. Cutting about 1/8" inside drawn line, cut shape from paper.

CELEBRATION CENTERPIECE

This spectacular party focal point (page 101) is a simple grouping of a few everyday items and party favorites that can be purchased at any party supply store. Carrying out the evening's theme, we used a black marker to write "PARTY" on a star cut from card stock paper and painted bright dots of acrylic paint on the star using the end of a paintbrush handle (for star, trace pattern, page 122, onto tracing paper and cut out; use pattern to cut star from card stock paper). We hot glued the decorated star to the handle of an ordinary gift bag and arranged the following items in the bag: pieces of cellophane, balloons on sticks with ribbons tied on, metallic shooting star sprays, and a party hat glued to a stick (for party hat, follow Party Hat Invitations instructions, page 108, cutting card from an unfolded piece of card stock paper and omitting Step 4).

To add to the fun, we filled two empty 12-ounce plastic beverage bottles with dried beans to add weight and wrapped each bottle with a piece of cellophane tied with assorted curling ribbons. More party hats and balloons on sticks, noise-makers, and metallic star sprays top off the containers.

DAZZLING PARTY GOBLETS

For each goblet (pages 100 and 101), you will need a clear acrylic goblet with colored stem (available at party supply stores), assorted acrylic jewels, and jewel glue.

Note: To maintain decorations, goblet must be hand washed.

Wash and dry goblet. Glue jewels to outside of goblet as desired.

PROM MEMORY BOOK

For each book (page 106), you will need a purchased autograph book (our book measures 6" x 4¹/₂"), fabric to cover book, card stock paper and assorted grosgrain ribbons to coordinate with fabric, a 4¹/₄" square of poster board, and craft glue.

Note: Frame on cover of book will hold a Polaroid® photograph or any other 3¹/₂" x 3" photograph.

1. To cover outside of book, measure length (top to bottom) and width of open book. Cut a piece of fabric ³/₄" larger on all sides than the determined measurements.
2. Center open book on wrong side of fabric piece. Fold corners of fabric diagonally over corners of book; glue in place. Fold short edges of fabric over side edges of book; glue in place. Fold long edges of fabric over top and bottom edges of book, trimming fabric to fit along top and bottom edges of book spine; glue in place.
3. To cover inside of book, cut 2 pieces of card stock paper slightly smaller than front of book. Glue paper pieces inside front and back of book.
4. For frame on front of book, use a pencil to draw a 2⁵/₈" x 3¹/₄" rectangle on poster board for frame opening (Fig. 1). Cut out frame opening.

Fig. 1

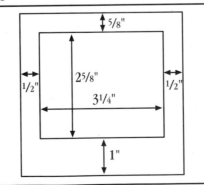

5. To cover frame, use pencil to lightly draw around frame and frame opening on wrong side of fabric. Cutting about ³/₈" from drawn lines, cut out fabric shape; at corners of opening in fabric, clip fabric to about ¹/₈" from drawn lines (Fig. 2).

Fig. 2

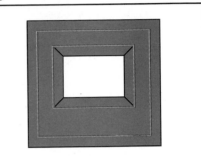

6. Center poster board frame on wrong side of fabric. Fold fabric edges at opening of frame to back; glue in place. Fold corners of fabric diagonally to back of frame (Fig. 3); glue in place. Fold remaining fabric edges to back of frame; glue in place.

Fig. 3

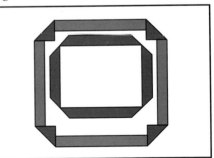

7. Cut four 5" lengths of ribbon. Center and glue 1 ribbon length along each side on right side of frame. Glue ribbon ends to back of frame.
8. Center frame on front of book and glue side and bottom edges of frame to book, leaving an opening at top for inserting photograph.
9. Tie several 1 yd lengths of ribbon together into a bow around front cover of book near binding; trim ends.

ANCHORS AWEIGH INVITATIONS

(Page 16)

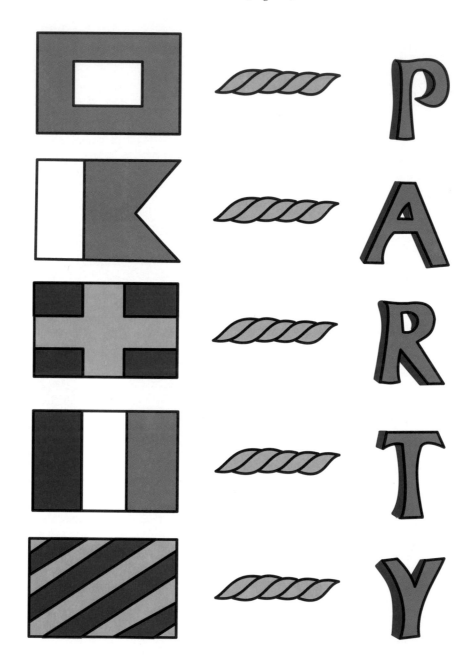

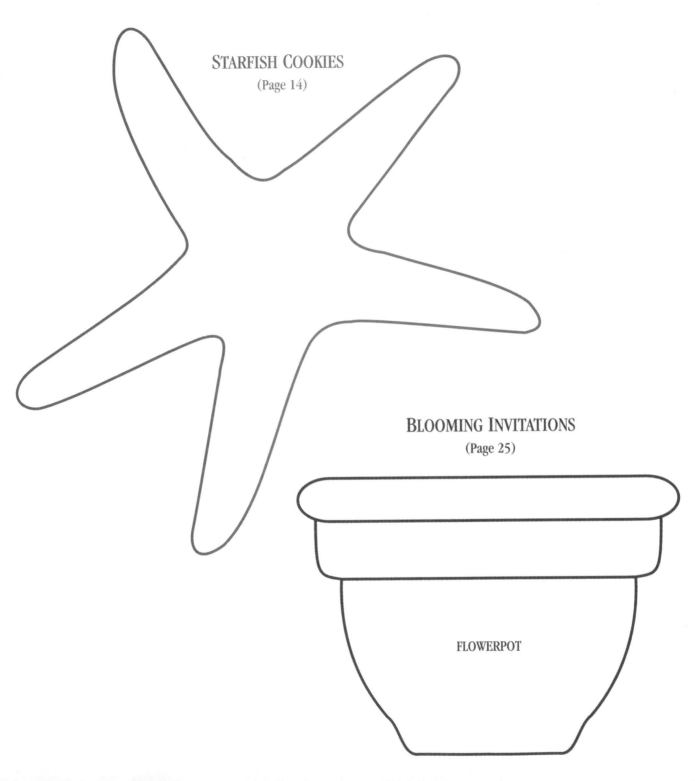

STARFISH COOKIES
(Page 14)

BLOOMING INVITATIONS
(Page 25)

FLOWERPOT

CENTERPIECE PENNANT

(Page 33)

A PAR JUST FORE! FUN

PATTERNS (continued)

TEAPOT CAKE
(Page 56)

SPOUT

"SOMEONE'S NESTING" INVITATIONS
(Page 52)

Someone's Nesting

HANDLE

TEACUP INVITATIONS
(Page 60)

it's a Tea Party!

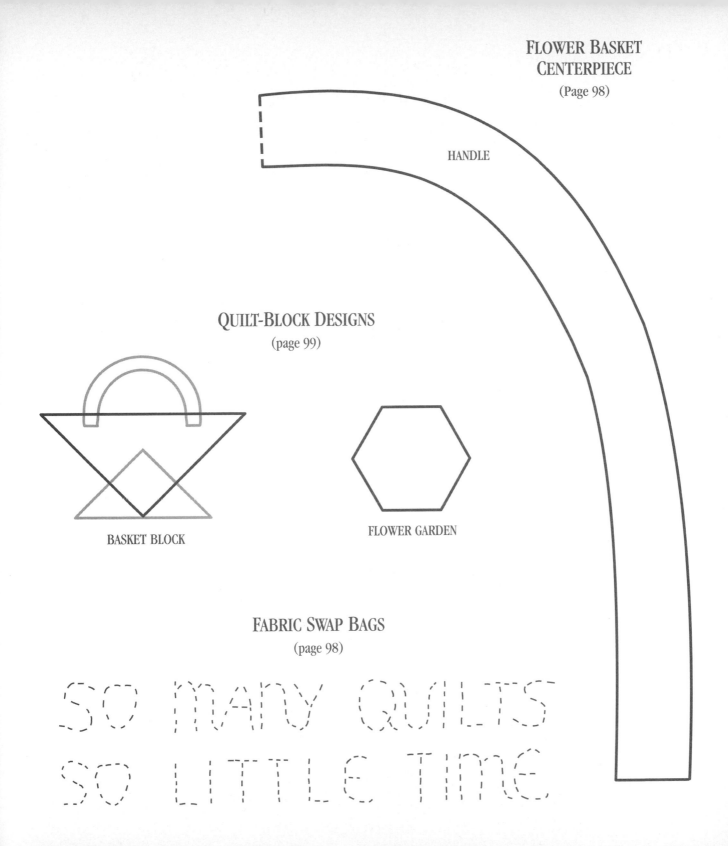

FLOWER BASKET
CENTERPIECE
(Page 98)

HANDLE

QUILT-BLOCK DESIGNS
(page 99)

BASKET BLOCK

FLOWER GARDEN

FABRIC SWAP BAGS
(page 98)

So many quilts
so little time

PATTERNS (continued)

You're Invited to a
"Wild" Birthday Party
at the Zoo.

For:

Date:

Time:

SAFARI LUNCH TOTES

(Page 67)

LION COLOR KEY
Basecoats
☐ white
▨ beige
▨ tan
▨ dark tan
■ dark brown
■ black
Details
◩ ◩ black

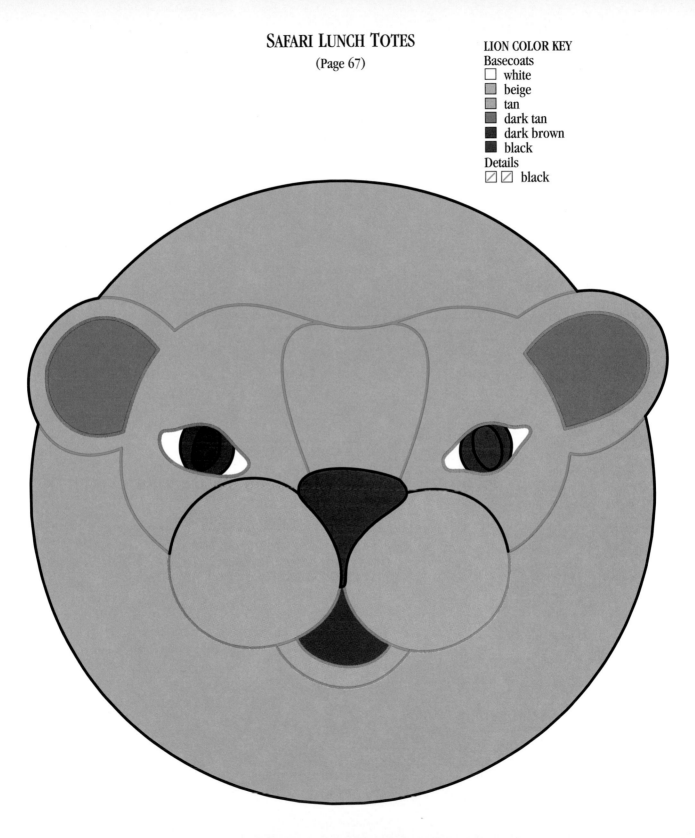

SAFARI LUNCH TOTES
(Page 67)
(Continued)

TIGER COLOR KEY
Basecoats
- yellow
- orange
- dark brown
- black

Details
☐ ☐ black

SAFARI LUNCH TOTES

(Page 67)
(Continued)

GIRAFFE COLOR KEY
Basecoats
gold
dark gold
brown
dark brown
black
Details
dark brown

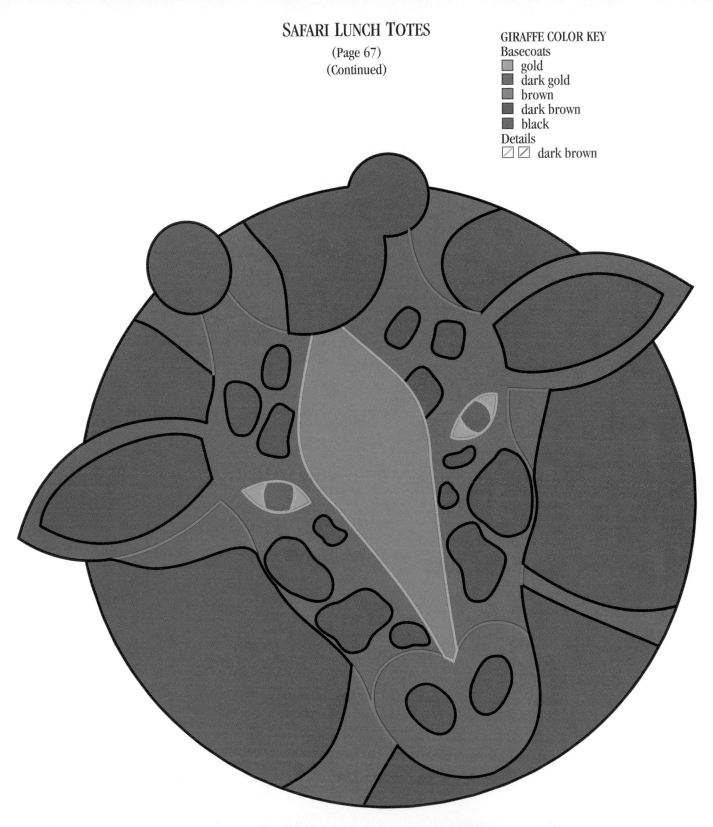

PATTERNS (continued)

HANDSAW INVITATIONS
(Page 86)

HANDLE

TOOLIN' TABLE DECOR
(Page 87)

A TOOL-TIME SHOWER

"GROOM"
HANDYMAN CAP
(Page 87)

GROOM

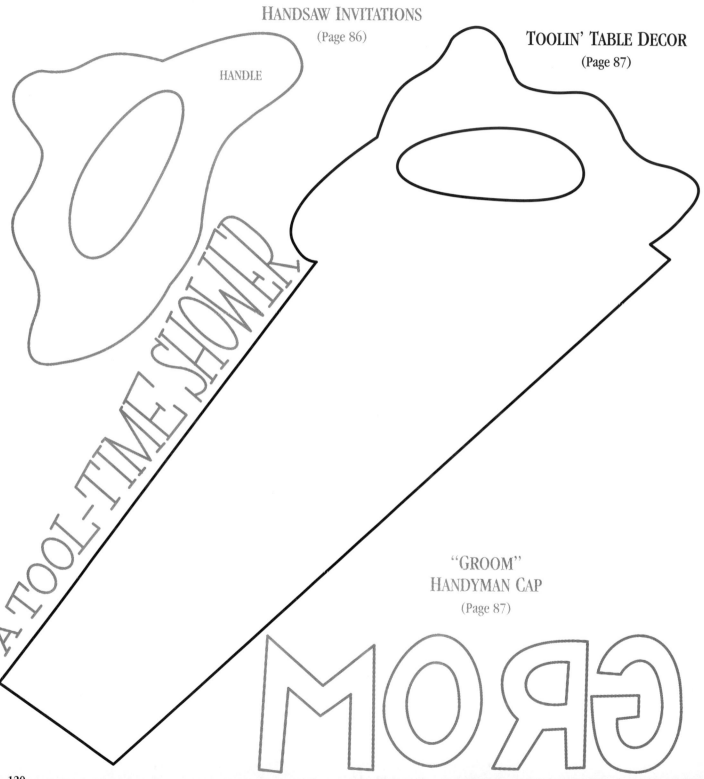

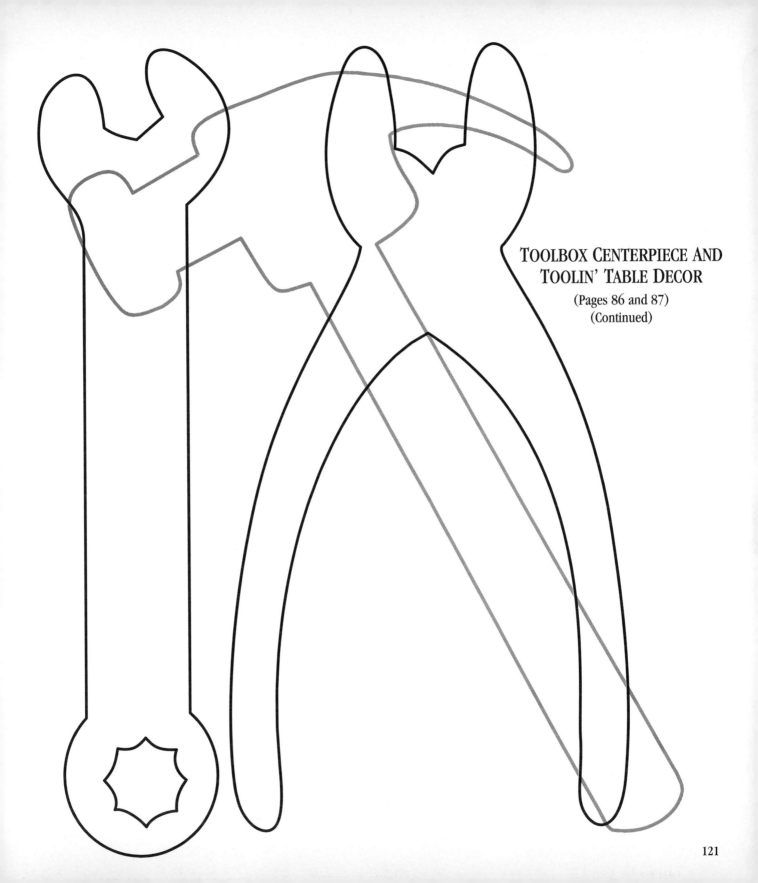

TOOLBOX CENTERPIECE AND
TOOLIN' TABLE DECOR
(Pages 86 and 87)
(Continued)

121

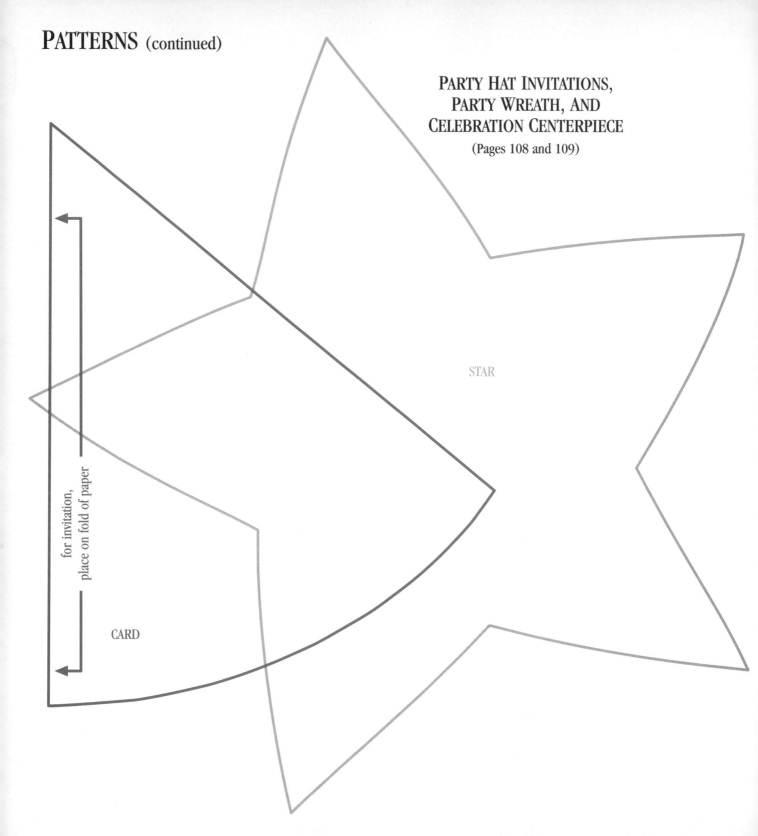

PARTY HAT INVITATIONS,
PARTY WREATH, AND
CELEBRATION CENTERPIECE
(Pages 108 and 109)

STAR

for invitation,
place on fold of paper

CARD

GENERAL INSTRUCTIONS

TRACING PATTERNS

When entire pattern is shown, place tracing paper over pattern and trace pattern; cut out. For a more durable pattern, use a permanent pen to trace pattern onto acetate; cut out.

When only half of pattern is shown (indicated by dashed line on pattern), fold tracing paper in half and place fold along dashed line of pattern. Trace pattern half; turn folded paper over and draw over traced lines on remaining side of paper. Unfold pattern and lay pattern flat; cut out. For a more durable pattern, use a permanent pen to trace pattern half onto acetate; turn acetate over and trace pattern half again, aligning dashed lines to form a whole pattern; cut out.

MAKING APPLIQUÉS

1. (*Note:* Follow all steps for each appliqué. When tracing patterns for more than 1 appliqué, leave at least 1" between shapes on fusible web. To make a reverse appliqué, trace pattern onto tracing paper, turn traced pattern over, and follow all steps using traced pattern.) Trace appliqué pattern onto paper side of web.

2. Cutting about 1/2" outside drawn lines, cut out web shape.

3. (*Note:* If using a lightweight fabric for appliqué over a dark or print fabric, follow manufacturer's instructions to fuse interfacing to wrong side of fabric before completing Step 3.) Follow manufacturer's instructions to fuse web shape to wrong side of fabric. Cut out shape along drawn lines.

MAKING A MULTI-LOOP BOW

1. For first streamer, measure desired length of streamer from 1 end of ribbon and gather ribbon between fingers (Fig. 1).

Fig. 1

2. For first loop, keep right side facing out and fold ribbon over to form desired size loop (Fig. 2). Repeat to form another loop same size as first loop (Fig. 3). Repeat to form desired number of loops. For remaining streamer, trim ribbon to desired length.

Fig. 2

Fig. 3

3. To secure bow, hold gathered loops tightly. Bring a length of wire around center of bow. Hold wire ends behind bow, gathering all loops forward; twist bow to tighten wire. Arrange loops as desired.

4. If bow center is desired, wrap a 6" length of ribbon around center of bow, covering wire and overlapping ends at back; trim excess. Hot glue to secure.

5. Trim ribbon ends as desired.

KITCHEN TIPS

MEASURING INGREDIENTS

Liquid measuring cups have a rim above the measuring line to keep liquid ingredients from spilling. Nested measuring cups are used to measure dry ingredients, butter, shortening, and peanut butter. Measuring spoons are used for measuring both dry and liquid ingredients.

To measure flour or granulated sugar: Spoon ingredient into nested measuring cup and level off with a knife. Do not pack down with spoon.

To measure confectioners sugar: Sift sugar, spoon lightly into nested measuring cup, and level off with a knife.

To measure brown sugar: Pack sugar into nested measuring cup and level off with a knife. Sugar should hold its shape when removed from cup.

To measure dry ingredients equaling less than 1/4 cup: Dip measuring spoon into ingredient and level off with a knife.

To measure butter, shortening, or peanut butter: Pack ingredient firmly into nested measuring cup and level off with a knife.

To measure liquids: Use a liquid measuring cup placed on a flat surface. Pour ingredient into cup and check measuring line at eye level.

To measure honey or syrup: For a more accurate measurement, lightly spray measuring cup or spoon with cooking spray before measuring so the liquid will release easily from cup or spoon.

TESTS FOR CANDY MAKING

To determine the correct temperature of cooked candy, use a candy thermometer and the cold water test. Before each use, check the accuracy of your candy thermometer by attaching it to the side of a small saucepan of water, making sure thermometer does not touch bottom of pan. Bring water to a boil. Thermometer should register 212 degrees in boiling water. If it does not, adjust the temperature range for each candy consistency accordingly.

When using a candy thermometer, insert thermometer into candy mixture, making sure thermometer does not touch bottom of pan. Read temperature at eye level. Cook candy to desired temperature range. Working quickly, drop about 1/2 teaspoon of candy mixture into a cup of ice water. Use a fresh cup of water for each test. Use the following descriptions to determine if candy has reached the correct consistency:

Soft Ball Stage (234 to 240 degrees): Candy can be rolled into a soft ball in ice water but will flatten when held in your hand.

Firm Ball Stage (242 to 248 degrees): Candy can be rolled into a firm ball in ice water but will flatten if pressed when removed from the water.

Hard Ball Stage (250 to 268 degrees): Candy can be rolled into a hard ball in ice water and will remain hard when removed from the water.

Soft Crack Stage (270 to 290 degrees): Candy will form hard threads in ice water but will soften when removed from the water.

Hard Crack Stage (300 to 310 degrees): Candy will form brittle threads in ice water and will remain brittle when removed from the water.

CUTTING DIAMOND SHAPES

To cut 1-inch-wide x 2 1/2-inch-long diamond-shaped pieces, start at 1 edge of pan and make 1-inch-wide cuts (Fig. 1).

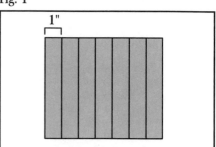

Fig. 1

Make a diagonal cut from lower left corner to upper right corner (shown by heavy black line). Make 1-inch-wide cuts on each side of first diagonal cut (Fig. 2).

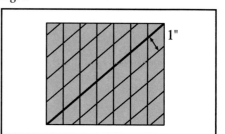

Fig. 2

TOASTING NUTS

To toast nuts, spread nuts on an ungreased baking sheet. Stirring occasionally, bake in a 350-degree oven 8 to 10 minutes or until nuts are slightly darker in color.

SMOOTHING BUTTERCREAM ICING

When a flat, smooth icing surface is desired, dip a knife or a long thin spatula in a glass of hot water. Wipe warm knife dry and use to smooth icing, warming knife between strokes.

PREPARING CITRUS FRUIT ZEST

To remove the zest (colored outer portion of peel) from citrus fruits, use a fine grater or fruit zester, being careful not to grate white portion of peel which is bitter.

ROLLING OUT PIE DOUGH

Use four 24-inch-long pieces of plastic wrap. Overlapping long edges, place 2 pieces of wrap on a slightly damp flat surface; smooth out wrinkles. Place dough in center of wrap. Overlapping long edges, use remaining pieces of wrap to cover dough. Use rolling pin to roll out dough 2 inches larger than diameter of pie plate. Remove top pieces of wrap. Invert dough into pie plate. Remove remaining pieces of wrap.

MELTING CHOCOLATE

To melt chocolate, place chopped or shaved chocolate in the top of a double boiler over hot, not boiling, water. Stir occasionally until chocolate melts. Remove from heat and use as desired. If necessary, chocolate may be returned to heat to remelt.

WHIPPING CREAM

For greatest volume, chill a glass bowl, beaters, and cream before whipping. In warm weather, place chilled bowl over ice while whipping cream.

SHREDDING CHEESE

To shred cheese easily, place wrapped cheese in freezer 10 to 20 minutes before shredding.

SOFTENING BUTTER OR MARGARINE

To soften 1 stick of butter, remove wrapper and place butter on a microwave-safe plate. Microwave on medium-low power (30%) 20 to 30 seconds.

SOFTENING CREAM CHEESE

To soften cream cheese, remove wrapper and place cream cheese on a microwave-safe plate. Microwave on medium power (50%) 1 to 1½ minutes for an 8-ounce package or 30 to 45 seconds for a 3-ounce package.

EQUIVALENT MEASUREMENTS

1 tablespoon	=	3 teaspoons
⅛ cup (1 fluid ounce)	=	2 tablespoons
¼ cup (2 fluid ounces)	=	4 tablespoons
⅓ cup	=	5⅓ tablespoons
½ cup (4 fluid ounces)	=	8 tablespoons
¾ cup (6 fluid ounces)	=	12 tablespoons
1 cup (8 fluid ounces)	=	16 tablespoons or ½ pint
2 cups (16 fluid ounces)	=	1 pint
1 quart (32 fluid ounces)	=	2 pints
½ gallon (64 fluid ounces)	=	2 quarts
1 gallon (128 fluid ounces)	=	4 quarts

HELPFUL FOOD EQUIVALENTS

½ cup butter	=	1 stick butter
1 square baking chocolate	=	1 ounce chocolate
1 cup chocolate chips	=	6 ounces chocolate chips
2¼ cups packed brown sugar	=	1 pound brown sugar
3½ cups unsifted confectioners sugar	=	1 pound confectioners sugar
2 cups granulated sugar	=	1 pound granulated sugar
4 cups all-purpose flour	=	1 pound all-purpose flour
1 cup shredded cheese	=	4 ounces cheese
3 cups sliced carrots	=	1 pound carrots
½ cup chopped celery	=	1 rib celery
½ cup chopped onion	=	1 medium onion
1 cup chopped green pepper	=	1 large green pepper

RECIPE INDEX

CREDITS

We want to extend a warm *thank you* to the generous people who allowed us to photograph our projects in their homes:

- *Anchors Aweigh Pool Party:* Mr. and Mrs. Layton Stuart
- *Summertime Supper:* Dr. Dan and Sandra Cook
- *Golfers' "Par-Tee":* Louis and Carolyn Schaufele

Special thanks go to the Hotze House Bed and Breakfast of Little Rock, Arkansas, for graciously allowing us to photograph the *Bridesmaids' Lovely Luncheon* section at the inn. We also thank the Little Rock Zoological Garden for allowing us to photograph the *"Zoo-pendous" Birthday Party* at the zoo.

To Magna IV Color Imaging of Little Rock, Arkansas, we say thank you for the superb color reproduction and excellent pre-press preparation.

We want to especially thank photographers Mark Mathews, Larry Pennington, Karen Shirey, and Ken West of Peerless Photography, Little Rock, Arkansas, and Jerry R. Davis of Jerry Davis Photography, Little Rock, Arkansas, for their time, patience, and excellent work.

We would also like to thank Viking Husqvarna Sewing Machine Company of Cleveland, Ohio, for providing the sewing machines used to make many of our projects.